Hertford
MURDERS

Nicholas Connell & Ruth Stratton

Sutton Publishing

First published in the United Kingdom in 2003 by
Sutton Publishing Limited · Phoenix Mill
Thrupp · Stroud · Gloucestershire · GL5 2BU

Series Consulting Editor: Stewart P. Evans

British Library Cataloguing in Publication Data
A catalogue record for this book is available from the British Library.

ISBN 0-7509-3330-5

Hertfordshire

For Richard Whittington-Egan

Typeset in 10.5/13.5 Sabon
Typesetting and origination by
Sutton Publishing Limited.
Printed and bound in England by
J.H. Haynes & Co. Ltd, Sparkford.

CONTENTS

ACKNOWLEDGEMENTS

The authors would like to thank the helpful staff of the British Library, the British Library Newspaper Library, Corporation of London Records Office, Hertford Museum, Hertfordshire Archives and Local Studies, Hertfordshire Central Resources Library, Public Record Office and St Albans Library.

We should also like to thank the following people for their help: our colleagues at Hertfordshire Archives and Local Studies, Margaret Ashby, Alex Chisholm, Susie Elliott, Stewart Evans, Ken Griffin, Stuart Lee, Jeremy McIlwaine, Sarah Moore, David Mossop, Hugh Noblett, Jon Ogan, Phil Sugden, Geoff Webb, Molly Whittington-Egan and Richard Whittington-Egan.

INTRODUCTION

The crime of murder has always held a macabre fascination. What drives a human being to slay a fellow creature in cold blood, a father to batter his sweetheart and child, a young man to butcher his fiancée and an unknown assailant to strangle an innocent seventeen-year-old girl and stash her body in a deep freeze? These are just some of the chilling true stories found in the pages of *Hertfordshire Murders*.

Hertfordshire is one of England's smallest counties yet it is crammed with a rich historical heritage; a county where fragments of a Roman past still linger and significant battles have been fought. Yet despite its proximity to London, Hertfordshire has retained its rural charm. With its scenic countryside, village curiosities and quiet woodland lanes, it has been the chosen residence of many royals and landed gentry in the past. It is no wonder this is still one of the most desirable counties in the South East. But not even this Home County idyll can escape the dark stain of murder.

Hertfordshire's murderous past is well documented in the county's records, but occasionally only a tantalising glimpse into a long-forgotten atrocity remains. The famous Hitchin historian Reginald Hine (1883–1949) noted that eight murders were committed in that historic market town in the year 1278 alone. The burial register for St Margaret's church, Barley, contains reference to a murder in 1598 of 'John Millisent of norwiche slaine in the fielde by one of the same cittye', leaving the reader hungry for more details about a story that will never now be told. More horrifying is an entry in the burial register of St Peter's church, Great Berkhamsted. On 17 March 1664 Robert Toefeild was buried, having been 'poysoned by his wife [who was later] burnt alive at Hertford'.

There have been a great number of murders in this county that caused a stir both locally and nationally. When newspapers became readily available in the early nineteenth century they spared little in satisfying the public's thirst for minute detail. This is best illustrated in Aldenham in 1823, when John Thurtell blasted his way into national notoriety with the killing of William Weare, thanks to the unparalleled coverage by the national press.

A collection of the most infamous cases in the county are examined in the following pages, using extensive sources from forgotten broadsheets to previously closed police files, witness statements and court transcripts. Some remain a mystery, but all are part of the murky criminal heritage of Hertfordshire.

A cruell murther committed lately

upon the body of Abraham Gearsy, who liv'd in the Parish of Westmill, in the County of Harford, by one Robert Reeve and Richard Reeve, both of the same Parish; for which fact Robert was prest to death on Monday, the 16 of March, and the Tuesday following Richard was hang'd; and after, both [of] them were hang'd up in chaines, where now they doe remaine, to the affrightment of all beholders, 1635.

To THE TUNE OF *Fortune, my foe.*

I pray give eare unto my tale of woe,
Which I'le declare, that all may plainly knowe:
Neare Harford lately was a murder done;
O! 'twas a cruell one as ever was knowne.

Illustration from a pamphlet detailing the murder of Abraham Gearsy at Westmill. The Westmill burial register has an entry for Abraham Gersy of Waterford in 1634. (HALS D/Ecu/2)

1

'SOME HERTFORDSHIRE TRAGEDIES'

Buried amid the prodigious collection of the great Hertfordshire antiquarian William Blyth Gerish (1864–1921) there is a 103-page manuscript entitled *Some Hertfordshire Tragedies*. It was written in 1913 when Gerish was living at Warwick Road, Bishops Stortford, and like too much of that worthy gentleman's work it never saw publication. The manuscript covers a variety of unpleasant and gruesome episodes in Hertfordshire's history including some unusual murder stories.

Gerish's first entry related to a skeleton uncovered during an archaeological dig at Hinxworth. The bones were believed to be those of a man who died aged about sixty over 10,000 years previously as a result of 'a tap from a flint axe on the top of his cranium'. Moving forward to the fifteenth century there was the story of James Roche, vicar of Sarratt in the Year of Grace 1462. The Register for the second Abbacy of John of Wheathampstead contained the following entry:

> On the 14th day of June the Vicarage of Saret [*sic*] was given to John Skeltone chaplain; the same being notoriously vacant because James Roche, the late vicar there, with his wicked abettors, namely, Roger Wittone, Esquire, and other strangers unknown, slew and murdered Richard Glowcestre, his parishioner, an artificer, with one Hogheler [another accomplice] and secretly buried him in a certain field belonging to the said Roger Wittone, on Sunday the 16th day of May, in the same year; and the said James Roche, who was vicar there, for this reason, took to flight.

Other finds unearthed by Gerish included a tract at the British Museum called *The Horrible Murther of a Young Boy of three years of age, whose Sister had her tongue cut out: and how it pleased God to reveal the offenders, by giving speech to the tongueless childe. Which Offenders were executed at Hartford the 4 of August, 1606.*

According to the tract this *cause célèbre* involved a boy and a girl who were staying at an inn and common lodging house in Hatfield kept by a couple named Dell. The boy's body was later found 'with a great peece of wood tyed to his backe', while his sister was discovered trapped in a hollow tree with her tongue cut out. The Dells were arrested but denied all knowledge of the murder and mutilation. They were bound over from one Assize court hearing to the next between 1602 and 1606. The girl had wandered the country in those years and in 1606 she found herself back in Hatfield where she miraculously regained the power of speech and gave evidence against the Dells at the Hertford Assizes. The Dells were subsequently found guilty of murder and mutilation by a jury who had earlier looked 'into the child's mouth, but could not see so much as the stumpe of a tongue therein'.

Confirmation that this story was based at least partly on true events can be found in the Assize calendar for 1 August 1606, at which date George Dell, a baker, and Agnes Dell, a widow, were indicted for the murder of Anthony James on 4 July 1602. George Dell had cut the boy's throat with a knife and thrown the body into a pond. Both Dells were sentenced to death.

The antiquarian William Blyth Gerish standing by the stocks and whipping post outside Brent Pelham church. Gerish was fascinated by all aspects of Hertfordshire's past, including murders. (HALS D/EGr/60)

While trawling the British Museum's collections for material relating to Hertfordshire, Gerish discovered another seventeenth-century pamphlet with an even grander title, *Save a thief from the gallows and he'll hang thee if he can; or the merciful Father and the merciless son. The confession and Repentance of George Sanders gent. Late of Sugh [sic] in the County of Hertford who killed his own Uncle and accused his own Father, but by God's Providence being discovered, dyed for the same, where he wrote this song with his own hand*. This pamphlet told the story of George Sanders in verse. The location of Sugh is uncertain as there has never been a place of that name in Hertfordshire.

Perhaps the most extraordinary case of murder described by Gerish was that of Johan or Joan Norkott. Details of the case were initially discovered among the papers of Sir John Maynard (1592–1658), Member of Parliament and former prisoner in the Tower of London.

According to Maynard, the incident took place during the fourth year of the reign of King Charles I (i.e. 1628–9). At the coroner's inquest on the body of Joan Norkott the jury heard depositions from Joan's mother-in-law Mary Norkott, her sister-in-law Agnes Okeman and her husband John Okeman. Their testimony seemed to indicate that Joan had committed suicide. However, rumours began to circulate that the evidence showed it would have been impossible for Joan to have killed herself.

It later emerged that Norkott's husband Arthur was absent on the night of her death but the other three defendants were all in the house. No one else had entered the house that night, so if Joan's death had not been a suicide then one or more of them must have murdered her. Norkott's throat had been cut from ear to ear and her neck was broken. She could have done one or the other to herself but not both. There was no blood on her bed except for a stain on the bolster where her head lay. There were two separate pools of blood on the floor indicating she had bled grievously in two different places in the room. The knife used was found sticking in the floor some distance from the bed.

The coroner's jury evidently had doubts and, as their verdict of *felo de se* (suicide), 'was not yet drawn unto form', they requested that Joan's body be exhumed. After re-examining the corpse the jury changed their mind and subsequently Mary Norkott, John and Agnes Okeman were tried for murder at the Hertford Assizes but found not guilty.

The judge felt that the verdict was greatly at odds with the evidence and let it be known that it would be better that an appeal be brought against the verdict rather 'than so foul a Murther escape unpunished'. Norkott's young son brought an appeal against his father (who was supposedly absent on the night of his wife's death), his grandmother and his aunt and uncle. Then:

[An] Ancient and Grave Person Minister to the Parish where the Fact was committed deposed that the Body being taken up out of the Grave

30 days after the parties Death; and lying on the Grass, and the four Defendants pressed, they were required each of them to touch the dead body. The Appallees did touch the Dead Body, whereupon the Brow of the Dead, which was before a Livid and Carrion Colour, began to have a Dew, or gentle Sweat arise on it, which increas'd by degrees, till the Sweat ran down in drops on the Face, the Brow turn'd and changed to a lively and Fresh Colour, and the Dead opened one of her Eyes, and shut it again; and this opening the Eye was done three several times; she likewise thrust out the Ring or Marriage Finger 3 times, and pulled it in again, and the Finger dropped Blood from it on the Grass.

By Maynard's account Mary Norkott, Agnes Okeman and Arthur Norkott were found guilty of murder. John Okeman was acquitted. Mary and Arthur Norkott were hanged. Agnes Okeman was spared the noose because she was pregnant.

It is impossible now to establish how much of Maynard's tale was true, particularly the veracity of the exhumation of the corpse and subsequent trial by ordeal, but the story was indubitably based on true events. At the Hertford Assizes of July 1623 a Thomas Norkett, his wife Mary and Agnes Okeman (the wife of John), all from Great Berkhamsted, were indicted for the murder of shovel maker John Norkett on 6 June 1623. Regrettably, much of the contemporary material has been lost or is illegible. Mary Norkett and Agnes Okeman were found not guilty but the verdict on Thomas Norkett is illegible.

The next entry in the Assize calendar shows indictments against John Okeman, John Norkett, Agnes Norkett, Arthur Norkett and Anne Andrewes possibly for the murder of John Norkett. The verdicts against them are unknown. The list of gaol prisoners at the March 1624 Assizes shows (with a slight difference in the spelling of names) that Thomas Norcott had died while John Okeman, Arthur Norcott, John Norcott, Mary Norcott, Agnes Okeman, Agnes Norcott and Anne Andrewes were all being held on remand at Hertford Gaol. Arthur at least was executed for the murder. There is a brief mention of his execution in a Berkhamsted manorial document dated 1627.

Gerish's book also contains several references to Hertfordshire's only city, St Albans, once known as Verulamium. It had been the third largest ancient Roman settlement in Britain after London and York. It was here in the third century that a Roman named Alban became the first Christian martyr when he was beheaded by his countrymen for giving shelter to a fleeing Christian. Gerish unearthed two pamphlets which told of a seventeenth-century murder in the cathedral city. It was more succinctly told by William Urwick in his 1884 work, *Nonconformity in Herts*.

In 1662 Nonconformist minister William Haworth preached at a funeral in the cloisters of St Albans Abbey. The congregation was interrupted by a Major Crosby who angrily called them rogues and rebels. He left, only to return soon afterwards brandishing a cocked pistol and accompanied by a constable bearing a fowling piece. Crosby was approached by congregation member John Townsend who entreated, 'Noble Major, pray make no disturbance; consider it is the Sabbath day.' A furious Crosby replied, 'You rogue, do you tell me of the Sabbath day?' before shooting Townsend dead on the spot.

A briefer tale was that of a family living at a farm in Hinxworth called the Vine. Early in the eighteenth century a band of highwaymen and gypsies robbed the farm and murdered the couple who lived there. Their daughter escaped death by hiding in a cupboard but their baby son was found asleep. A gypsy woman wrapped him in a shawl and placed him close to the hearth and said, 'If thou should'st live to be a man, say Rose of Royston wrapt thee warm.' The robbers left their black dog behind at the farm. The dog was followed home to Royston where its owners were found and hanged.

It was not only in old books and documents that Gerish found evidence of early Hertfordshire murders. He had previously spent years recording monumental inscriptions in churchyards and burial grounds throughout the county. In Walkern churchyard he found an altar tomb that read:

Here lyeth interred the body of Thomas Adams, gent, late of this parish, who was barbarously murdered the 21st December, 1728 on his return from Hertford market, aged thirty-eight years.

Gerish stated that Adams's murderer was never discovered but attributed the crime to 'a man of bad repute living in Hertford'. In fact, Richard Curral was tried for the murder of Adams on the evidence of a man named William Newton but was acquitted. Ironically, on 21 March 1732 Curral and Newton stood side by side on the gallows at Hertford having been found guilty of highway robbery and burglary respectively. Their behaviour at the scene of the execution was described by observers as 'uncommonly rude'.

At the end of his manuscript of *Some Hertfordshire Tragedies* William Gerish concluded that 'it has recorded many events of importance connected with the history of the county, and to the student of the past may not be without value'. It is hoped the same may be said of the following accounts in *Hertfordshire Murders*.

2

THE TRIAL OF SPENCER COWPER

Hertford, 1699

One of the most enduring mysteries in the annals of Hertfordshire's history is how did Sarah Stout die? Her body was found in a Hertford millstream in 1699. Had she been driven to commit suicide, tormented by her unrequited love for the married barrister Spencer Cowper? Or had Cowper, together with several colleagues, conspired to murder her?

Spencer Cowper (pronounced Cooper) was a member of a well-known Whig family. His father and brother (both named William) represented the borough of Hertford in Parliament. Among those who supported the Cowpers during elections were the Stouts, a wealthy Quaker family.

The day of the Spring Assizes, 13 March 1699, brought into Hertford members of the legal profession including Spencer Cowper. Cowper had previously lodged with the Stouts during the Hertford Assizes and his wife had written to them on the Friday before the Assizes telling them to expect him. He initially called in at Mr Barefoot's house in Hertford. Barefoot offered the best accommodation in town and Cowper's brother William usually stayed there when attending the Assizes. On this occasion William had been detained in London on parliamentary business and had forgotten to cancel his rooms. Knowing that Barefoot's rooms would have to be paid for whether they were used or not, Cowper decided to stay there. He sent his horse to the Stouts' for stabling along with a note explaining he would be staying at Mr Barefoot's instead.

Cowper did visit the Stouts' house to dine and to give Sarah Stout an interest payment on £200 he had invested on her behalf the previous year. She appeared to think, or perhaps hope, that Cowper was staying with them for she instructed her maid Sarah Walker to warm a bed for him at around 11 p.m. Walker said she heard the house door slam at around 11.15. The Stouts' clock was half an hour fast so Cowper had in fact left the house at 10.45. Walker went downstairs and found Cowper and Sarah both gone. Both she and Sarah's mother sat up all night expecting Sarah to return but she never did.

Earlier that day, at around 5 p.m., two other men had also arrived in Hertford. Ellis Stephens and William Rogers were attorneys and in Hertford for the Assizes. They arranged lodgings at the house of John, Matthew and Elizabeth Gurrey and then went to a coffee house where they met a scrivener named John Marson at around 8 p.m. The three then went to the Glove and Dolphin inn, returning to the Gurreys' at 11 p.m. There was no spare room for Marson, who seemed to be unusually hot, but the Gurreys agreed to allow him to share the room with Stephens and Rogers.

The three lodgers called for wine and for a fire to be started in their room. While the Gurreys were doing this they allegedly heard the trio gossiping about Sarah Stout. When one of them referred to Stout as being an old sweetheart of Marson's he replied, 'Ay, but she cast me off, but I reckon a friend of mine is even with her by this time.' Another was heard to say, 'Well, her business is done, Mrs Sarah Stout's courting days are over.' One of them pulled out a wad of money, some £40 or £50 according to the Gurreys, saying, 'I will spend all the money I have, for joy the business is done.'

At around 6 a.m. on Tuesday 14 March mill owner James Berry saw some clothes floating on the surface of the water of the Priory River. Upon closer examination he realised that the clothes were on the body of a woman just beneath the surface of the water, which was around five feet deep. The body was lying on its side and the eyes were wide open and staring, the teeth clenched. Quantities of froth 'like the froth of new beer' were emerging from the corpse's mouth and nostrils. It was also observed that her shoes and stockings were not muddy.

The body was soon identified as Sarah Stout. It was removed from the water and placed in a meadow before being taken to a nearby barn. Over six guineas were found in her clothing – the interest payment she had received from Cowper the previous night. Local surgeon John Dimsdale was called to examine the corpse. Dimsdale was not very interested. As the woman was dead there was nothing he could do about it. It was not until he was asked for a third time that he went to view the body. Dimsdale saw swelling on her neck and marks or bruises between her breasts and near her collarbone.

Coincidentally, some ten weeks earlier the body of a girl aged about ten or eleven had been found drowned in the same place. Like Stout she had been discovered after spending a night in the water. Witnesses who had seen both corpses noticed some striking differences. The girl's body was found at the bottom of the river. Her eyes were shut and, unlike Stout, her body was swollen with water.

At a coroner's inquest Dimsdale described the swelling on Stout's neck as 'a settling of blood on both sides of the neck', adding that such stagnation of blood was normal in cases like this one. As Cowper appeared to be the last person to have seen Sarah Stout alive, the coroner questioned him. Cowper described Sarah as a very modest woman and knew of no reason why she would have drowned herself. The jury returned the verdict that Stout had committed suicide while *non compos mentis*.

Rogers, Stephens and Marson had left Hertford on the 14th and went to stay at The Bull in Hoddesdon. A piece of cord was found in their room at the Gurreys' (it would later be suggested that it had been used to strangle Sarah Stout). Cowper left on the 15th and went to Chelmsford where the Essex Assizes were to be held.

At the behest of her family, Sarah Stout's corpse was exhumed on 28 April to dispel circulating rumours that she had been pregnant and Cowper was the father. Several doctors examined the rotting cadaver and found that she was not pregnant. One of the doctors had been told there was some suspicion that Stout had been murdered. They found no water in her intestines, stomach, lungs or diaphragm. This came as some surprise to the doctors who expected to find Stout's internal organs rotted away by swallowed water. Instead her 'stomach and guts were as full of wind as if they had been blown with a pair of bellows'.

After completing the post-mortem the doctors had a consultation to discuss whether, contrary to the coroner's verdict, Stout had not drowned after all. The absence of water in Stout's body led them to conclude that she had not. Surgeon John Dimsdale recalled, 'we were all of opinion that she was not drowned'. His colleague Mr Coatsworth had once narrowly escaped drowning himself and said, 'This woman could not be drowned, for if she had taken in water, the water must have rotted all the guts; that was the construction I made of it then; but for any marks about the head or neck, it was impossible for us to discover it, because they were so rotten.'

Rumours now became more widespread that Sarah Stout had been murdered. Spencer Cowper had been the last person seen with her and Stephens, Rogers and Marson had spoken of her in strange terms. The four men were summoned by Chief Justice Holt who twice questioned them. Stephens, Rogers and Marson were bailed but Cowper was remanded in custody until the next Assize.

All four men stood trial for the murder of Sarah Stout at the Hertford Summer Assizes in 1699. The trial was the most high-profile case that the judge, Baron Henry Hatsell, was to hear in his unspectacular legal career. Cowper elected to defend himself and his fellow defendants. The prosecutor was a Mr Jones.

Jones declared Stout had been murdered. Her death was 'one of the foulest and most wicked crimes almost that any age can remember . . . a murder accompanied with all the circumstances of wickedness that I remember in all my practice or ever read of'. Jones viewed the proceedings as two trials. The first was to vindicate Stout's reputation against the claims she had committed suicide. The second was to find the defendants guilty of her murder.

Jones stated there was no motive for suicide and suggested that the marks seen on Stout's neck when she was removed from the river indicated she had been strangled by hands or a rope. However, it appeared that Jones's case was

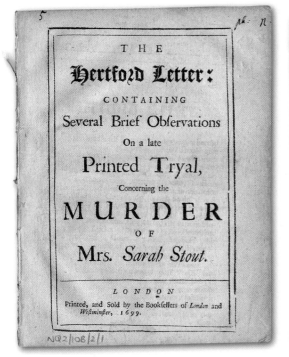

Examples of pamphlets published after Spencer Cowper's acquittal. Some vilified him as a murderer, others defended him. (HALS NQ2/10B/2/1)

not as strong as he would have liked. At the outset he told the jury that, 'The thing was done in the dark, therefore the evidence cannot be so plain as otherwise might be.'

The prosecution's first goal was to try to prove that Stout had been killed and thrown into the river rather than having drowned herself. To do this, Jones argued that Stout's body had been floating in the river when it was discovered. He explained, 'if persons come alive into the water, then they sink; if dead, then they swim [i.e. float]'. Jones called several witnesses who had seen her body in the water and said it was floating. A number of doctors also gave evidence. They all agreed with Jones's argument that drowned bodies sink, adding that they would have expected to find a lot of water in her body if she had drowned.

Then sailors were called to give evidence. One named Edward Clement had fought the French at the Battle of Beachy Head in 1690. He regaled the court with yarns about his shipmates who had died at sea. He concluded: 'We hold it for a general rule, that all men swim [float] if they be dead before they come into the water; and on the contrary, I have seen men when they had been drowned, that they have sunk as soon as the breath was out of their bodies, and I could see no more of them.'

Mr Jones said that the evidence presented so far proved that Sarah Stout had not committed suicide therefore she must have been dead when she entered the water. He then tried to prove the four defendants were guilty of murder. He questioned why Marson was in such a hot state and wearing wet and dirty boots when he arrived at the Gurreys' house. Marson's answer was a little unconvincing. He said that he had ridden forty miles from Southwark that day. However, he had arrived at Hertford at 8 p.m. and spent several hours at the Glove and Dolphin with Stephens and Rogers. Even after three hours at the inn he claimed not to have cooled down.

Spencer Cowper now presented the case for the defence. He began by saying there was no positive evidence against them, only supposition and inference. It had been an 'unfortunate accident' that he had been the last person seen with Stout but: 'I did not in the least imagine that so little, so trivial an evidence as here is, could possibly have affected me to so great a degree, as to bring me to this place to answer for the worst fact that the worst of men can be guilty of.'

In Cowper's opinion, the prosecution had been instigated by his family's political rivals the Tories, 'to destroy, or break at least, the interest of my family in this place', and the Quakers, 'to maintain the reputation of their sect'. Cowper railed against the Quakers:

> For they think it is a wonderful thing, nay, absolutely impossible (however other people may be liable to such resolutions,) that one who was by her education entitled to the 'light within her,' should run headlong into the water, as if she had been possessed by the devil; of this they think their sect is to be cleared, though by spilling the blood of four innocent men.

Cowper said he would prove Sarah Stout had committed suicide. He opened his defence by explaining: 'The first fact that they insisted upon to infer a murder from it, was, that the body was found floating . . . for the fact was directly otherwise, that is, she was not found floating . . . she lay sideways between the stakes, and almost all under water.'

This was supported by a number of witnesses who had seen Stout's body in the river. Cowper had a team of ten medical witnesses, several of whom had spent the previous night drowning numerous dogs to ascertain whether they floated or sank. These doctors refuted the prosecution's claim that dead bodies float, saying that bodies placed in water when dead sank. The unfortunate canines were also dissected and little water was found in their stomachs. Cowper explained, 'sometimes drowned bodies are swelled more, sometimes less, sometimes not at all.'

Judge Hatsell questioned one of the witnesses, Dr Garth, who had confidently asserted that dead animals sink when placed in water. Hatsell pointed out that the sailors had said that when dead bodies were thrown overboard, 'if you do not tye a weight to them, they will not sink what say you to that?' Garth responded, 'the design of tying weights to their bodies, is to prevent their floating at all, which otherwise would happen in some few days.'

A crucial part of Cowper's defence was the time he entered the Glove and Dolphin inn after leaving Stout's house. He arrived there as the town clock struck eleven. The inn was around a quarter of a mile from the Stouts' house. It would have taken Cowper at least half an hour to get from the house to the Priory River and then back to the Glove and Dolphin. However, he had left the Stouts' around 10.45 and arrived at the inn some fifteen minutes later and he stayed for a further fifteen minutes.

Cowper then presented evidence to show that Sarah Stout had been suffering from depression at the time of her death. He apologised for resorting to these tactics but he was defending himself against a charge of murder and his life was at stake. Sarah Walker denied that Sarah was depressed but admitted that her mistress had been ill and suffered from severe headaches for the past twelve months which made her melancholic. Other witnesses gave compelling evidence that they had recently seen Stout in a melancholic state. Elizabeth Toller recalled how Stout said 'she would drown herself'. Cowper's sister-in-law recalled a time when Stout had a fever, 'and she said she was in great hopes it would end her days; and that she neglected herself in doing those things that were necessary for her health, in hopes it would carry her off, and often wished herself dead.'

It was believed that the cause of Stout's depression was that she was in love with someone, but she would not say with whom other than it was a man she could not marry. Cowper thought that a man called Thomas Marshall was courting her. Marshall, having heard 'the report of the world as to her fortune', did make a half-hearted attempt to woo her. Stout gave Marshall 'frequent opportunities of improving that acquaintance', but he soon received 'a very fair denial, and there ended my suit'.

Marshall later said that Cowper told him he 'ought to be thankful I had no more to do with her'. Perhaps Cowper's wariness of Stout arose from an occasion when he asked Stout about her courtship with Marshall. 'Do you imagine I intend to marry Mr Marshall?' Stout asked. She then told Cowper that she was only seeing Marshall because she 'thought it might serve to divert the censure of the world, and favour our acquaintance'. Cowper then produced a number of letters Stout had written. One of them had been sent to Cowper and included the line, 'for come life, come death, I am resolved never to desert you'.

The evidence against Stephens, Rogers and Marson was too flimsy to stand up to scrutiny. They had stayed in the Glove and Dolphin until around 11 p.m. and witnesses could confirm this. They flatly denied saying the things about

Sarah Stout which had been attributed to them. The £40 or £50 they were supposed to have been waving about was in fact just fifty shillings that Marson had earned from a case at Southwark.

Hatsell's summing up and handling of the case has been much criticised over the centuries. During the trial Hatsell referred to a book concerning dead bodies floating, unhelpfully saying, 'I do not understand it myself, but he hath a whole chapter about it.' After both sides had presented their evidence, Hatsell addressed the jury:

> Gentlemen, I was very much puzzled in my thoughts, and was at a loss to find out what inducement there could be to draw in Mr. Cowper, or these three other gentlemen, to commit such a horrid, barbarous, murder. And on the other hand, I could not imagine what there should be to induce this gentlewoman, a person of plentiful fortune, and a very sober good reputation, to destroy herself.

It was all too much for Hatsell who admitted, 'I know not what to make of it . . . I am a little faint, and cannot remember any more of the evidence.' All four men were found not guilty of the murder of Sarah Stout.

The populace of Hertford had followed the case closely and afterwards conducted their own experiment which was recorded in the pages of a journal called the *Postman*:

> They write from *Hartford*, [sic] that on *Saturday* last, one William Ricles was hanged for Burglary, and afterwards stripped and flung into the River, wherein the late Mrs *Stout* was drowned, this was done in the presence of several hundreds, and the Body immediately sunk to the Bottom, it was several times raised to the surface, but still sunk, afterwards it was taken out, but no water purged from the Nose, Mouth, Eyes, Ears, or any other part, as it did in the case of Mrs *Stout*. This experiment was made by the people, it having been insisted on at the late Tryal against Mr. Cowper that all bodies dead before they are thrown in the Water would float, but so many hundreds having seen experiment with their own eyes, the opinions of the Surgeons produced on the part of the King is thereby destroyed and exploded, and all persons convinced of the contrary.

In the years following Spencer Cowper's acquittal, a number of pamphlets appeared that commented on the trial. They represented the views of both Cowper's supporters and his critics. It was rumoured that the Cowper family bought up as many as they could in order to destroy them.

The trial did not stop Cowper becoming a Member of Parliament in 1705. He was later made attorney general to the Prince of Wales (the future King

The memorial to Spencer Cowper in the Cowper chapel at Hertingfordbury church. (Authors' Collection)

George I). After becoming the Chief Justice of Chester in 1717 Cowper achieved the pinnacle of his professional life in 1727, when he was promoted to the office of Judge of Common Pleas.

Spencer Cowper died in December 1728 and was buried at Hertingfordbury. He is today remembered as being the grandfather of the poet William Cowper, but the old scandal remained with the family for decades. When Cowper's descendants took up political careers, their appearances at hustings were often met with cries of 'Who killed the Quaker?'

3

THE GUBBLECOTE WITCH KILLING

Tring, 1751

'*Thou shalt not suffer a witch to live*' (Exodus 22: 18), declared the 1604 edition of the King James Bible, and the subsequent 'Witchcraze' which swept through Britain in the sixteenth and seventeenth centuries cost the lives of thousands. By the middle of the seventeenth century the mania had started to decline; the Age of Enlightenment dawned with education and learning replacing the dark superstitious beliefs of medieval times and scientific explanations were sought for the origin of the universe.

But belief in witchcraft lingered on in country districts and in 1712 in Hertfordshire Jane Wenham of Walkern was the last woman to be tried and condemned to death in England. She was pardoned by Queen Anne and was allowed to live out her natural life in peace. But such was the notoriety of her trial, occurring in an age of justice and reason, that it did much to bring about the repeal of the Witchcraft Act in 1736, demonstrating a growing move away from belief in magic. Witchcraft would no longer carry the death penalty, but would be punishable by imprisonment.

Hertfordshire was again the centre of a national sensation concerning witchcraft in 1751. A little hamlet near Tring witnessed the last recorded punishment of a witch in Britain. The method used was 'witch swimming', an old test for those accused of witchcraft. The witch was guilty if she floated, innocent if she sank. The unfortunates involved in this case were John and Ruth Osborn.[†]

Six years previously Ruth Osborn, a poor woman in her late sixties, had gone to a man named Butterfield who kept a dairy at the hamlet of Gubblecote near Tring. Ruth begged him for some buttermilk but the dairyman brutally refused her, telling her he didn't have enough to feed his hogs. Ruth went away muttering and cursing Butterfield, saying that the 'Pretender would pay him out'. The year was 1745, a little before the defeat of the Scots in the rebellion for the Pretender, Bonnie Prince Charlie, whom many thought was in league with the devil.

---

† Some sources spell the name as Osborne.

14

Soon afterwards, several of Butterfield's calves became distempered and the dairyman was convinced old mother Osborn had bewitched him. To try and rid himself of the curse Butterfield left his dairy business and took on a nearby public house by Gubblecote brook. There he became troubled by fits and, even though he had experienced them some years before, Ruth Osborn was believed to be the cause.

It appears that the doctors could not help Butterfield and he was persuaded to send for a white witch in Northamptonshire who was famous for curing diseases brought on by malevolent witchcraft. She confirmed that Butterfield had indeed been bewitched by one who practised the black arts and prescribed that six men watch his house day and night with staves and pitchforks, wearing protective charms about their necks.

But Butterfield continued fitting and, bent on revenge, whipped up the support of hard-drinking men who regularly patronised his alehouse. Then on 18 April 1751 a man named Nichols went to William Dell, the crier of Hemel Hempstead, and handed him four pence and an ominous unsigned piece of paper. The crier accordingly announced that 'On Monday next, a man and a woman are to be publicly ducked at Tring, in this county, for their wicked crimes.' This notice was also given at Winslow and Leighton Buzzard in Bedfordshire and came to the attention of Matthew Barton, parish overseer of Tring. When he discovered the unfortunates in this case were John and Ruth Osborn, he became fearful for their safety. These were two innocent old people. Barton removed the Osborns from their home and sent them to the workhouse as protection from the angry mob that was beginning to gather in the village.

Monday 22 April arrived and with it an immense number of people, reported to be around five thousand. Not all were from the lower classes; several were said to be mounted on horseback and others were substantial farmers. Between about 11 a.m. and midday the crowd came armed with pitchforks and sticks, vowing revenge against the 'wizard and witch' and demanding the couple be brought to them. Leading the mob was a local chimney sweep by the name of Thomas Colley. He called upon John Tomkins, master of the workhouse, to bring the couple out of hiding. But on the preceding evening Tomkins, anticipating violence, had removed the Osborns to the vestry room of the church for safety. Colley, fuelled by alcohol, refused to believe this and viciously threatened Tomkins before inciting the mob who smashed the windows, broke down the doors and rushed in to ransack the workhouse.

They pulled down a wall and in their fury even searched for the couple in salt boxes, a space that would have barely contained a cat. But such was the ignorance and superstition of the crowd that they believed the old woman capable of transforming herself into a creature of such size. Colley then noticed a hole in the ceiling and demanded a search be made in the rafters. But when the old couple were still not found, the mob turned on Tomkins. Their blood was up and they threatened to set fire to the house and burn it

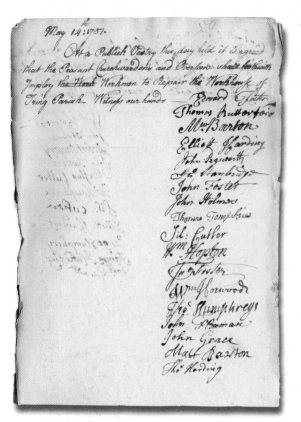

down if the couple's whereabouts was not revealed. Others cried that they would not be satisfied with burning down the workhouse but swore to reduce the whole of the town to ashes.

More people had joined the crowd by this time, all strangers to the village and none who knew the accused. A stone was flung at the window and then several more until every window in the house was broken and most of the lower windows and frames were entirely demolished. One brick end of the house was pulled down and a garden fence and wall were destroyed. Tomkins was terrified that they would carry out their threats to raze the village and finally admitted where the couple were hiding.

Order of the Vestry to repair Tring Workhouse after it had been damaged in the riots of 1751. (HALS D/P 111/8/18)

The entire mob, with Colley at its head, swarmed over to the church and broke open the vestry room door. On finding their quarry cowering in the corner, the mob was triumphant and the couple were snatched up into the fury and mayhem. In a moment they were stripped naked and separately wrapped in a cloth or sheet with a rope tied under the armpits. Ruth was carried like a calf across the shoulders of Charles 'Red Beard' Young for two miles until they reached a pond at Marlston Green. The couple separately had their big toes and thumbs tied together and Colley dragged Ruth into the pond by the rope, where she remained for nearly three quarters of an hour. Then, after she had been dragged around the pond several times, she was turned on her face but she did not sink, which provided further proof to the crowd that she was indeed a witch.

After a considerable time, and jeered on by the crowd, Ruth was hauled on to the muddy bank and left to lie there while her husband was put to the test. John Osborn fared no better. Both the old people were subjected to this barbarous trial three times, forced to endure the baying of the mob and the endless prodding of Colley's stick as he turned their trussed bodies over and over in the cold murky waters of the pond. At one point the sheet that had been wrapped around Ruth slipped off and her naked body was exposed to the mob. Colley

The last witch swimming in the country, that of Ruth Osborn, Tring, 1751. (HALS D/EGr 76)

continued to push her on the breast with his stick and Ruth suddenly reached out and with her left hand endeavoured to catch hold of the weapon and snatch it away. It was her last spirited act as soon after her body floated motionless on the water. Her tormentor finally dragged her corpse to the bank, but continued kicking and prodding it even though she was dead.

Colley, fired up by adrenaline, went among the spectators and collected money for the pains he had taken in showing them sport in ducking the old witch. John Osborn survived the ordeal but, to add to the barbarity, he was taken back to his home where he was laid on his bed next to the dead body of his wife. Some reports say they were tied together. He died several days later.

The body of Ruth Osborn was examined by Mr Foster, a surgeon, who declared that cause of death was suffocation with water and mud. The pond where she lost her life was not more than two and a half feet deep.

Of the violent mass mob involved in this case only the ringleader, Thomas Colley, could feasibly be brought to justice. On 30 July 1751 at the Hertford Assizes before Sir Thomas Lee, Colley was condemned for the murder of Ruth Osborn. He stated:

> I happened to be so unfortunate as to be at Marlston Green, among other people, out of curiosity to see what the mob would do with John Osborn and his wife; where, seeing that they used them very barbarously, I went into the pond as a friend, to save her if I could; for I knew both very well and never had any occasion to fall out with them, but bore them good will. As for the money I collected by the pondside, it was for the great pains I had taken in the pond to save both the man and the woman.

Conversely, Colley also said he had not intended to kill Ruth, just to carry out a fair trial by 'swimming' in the old tradition. From his confessions it appeared Colley had learned of 'witch swimming' from a previous case in the neighbouring county of Bedfordshire some sixteen years before. He believed that 'swimming' was a legally accepted process. Despite the number of people who had joined Colley in torturing the old couple, no witnesses came forward to support him at his trial.

The court was unanimous that he was the murderer of an innocent old woman and it determined to dispel local sympathy for the rioters and make an example. Colley was found guilty of wilful murder, much to the displeasure of the population.

In the dawn light of 24 August 1751 Colley was escorted from Hertford Gaol by two troops of horse guards, comprising nearly 120 men. Around 11 a.m., he reached the place of execution at Gubblecote Cross where his wife and daughter came to say their final goodbyes to him. Here he was hanged, near to where his crime had taken place. His body was then hung in chains on the same gallows. Many refused to be spectators of his death. Those that did

Good People I beseech you all to take Warning by an unhappy Man's suffering, that you be not deluded into so absurd & wicked a Conceit, as to believe that there are any such Beings upon Earth as Witches.

It was that Foolish & vain Imagination, heighten'd & inflamed by the strength of Liquor, which prompted me to be instrumental (with Others as mad-brain'd as my self) in the horrid & barbarous Murther of Ruth Osborn, the supposed Witch; for which I am now so deservedly to suffer Death.

I am fully convinced of my former Error and with the Sincerity of a dying Man declare that I do not believe there is such a Thing in Being as a Witch: And I pray God that None of you, thro' a contrary Perswasion, may hereafter be induced to think that you have a Right in any shape to persecute, much less endanger the Life of a Fellow-Creature.

I beg of you all to pray to God to forgive me & to wash clean my polluted Soul in the Blood of Jesus Christ my Saviour, & Redeemer.

So Exhorteth you all the Dying

Sign'd at Hertford aug.^t the 23. 1751 — Thomas Colley
just after Receiving the Sacrament
In Presence of Edw: Bouchier — Minister } of all Saints
    Robt Keep — Parish Clerk

The signed declaration of Thomas Colley, perpetrator of the witch killing at Tring in 1751, just before his execution. (HALS D/ELw/Z22/13)

stood at a distance grumbling that it was a sad sign of the times when a 'witch swimming' was no longer a fit sport for the public and that it was a hard case to hang a man for destroying a wicked old woman who had done so much mischief by her witchcraft.

On the day before his execution Colley had received the sacrament and signed the following solemn declaration, which he requested be circulated around several towns and villages in the county:

> Good People I beseech you all to take Warning by
> an unhappy Man's suffering, that you be not
> deluded into so absurd & wicked a Conceit, as to
> believe that there are any such Beings upon
> Earth as Witches.
>
> It was That Foolish & vain Imagination,
> heighten'd & inflamed by the strength of Liquor
> which prompted me to be instrumental
> (with others as mad-braind as myself) in
> the horrid & barbarous Murther of Ruth
> Osborn, the supposed Witch; for which I am
> now so deservedly to suffer Death.
>
> I am fully convinced of my former Error –
> and with the sincerity of a dying Man declare
> that I do not believe there is such a
> Thing in Being as a Witch: and I pray
> God that none of you, thro' a contrary
> Perswasion, may hereafter be induced to think
> that you have a Right in any shape to
> persecute, much less endanger the Life of a
> Fellow-Creature.
>
> I beg of you all to pray to God to forgive me
> & to wash clean my polluted soul in the Blood
> of Jesus Christ, my Saviour, & Redemer.
>
> So Exhorteth you all the Dying
> Thomas Colley

This may have been the last 'witch swimming' in Britain, but it was not the end of belief in witches in the county of Hertfordshire. With Colley held up as a martyr by many of the population, county historian Robert Clutterbuck wrote in 1815 that the belief in witchcraft was still strong in the neighbourhood and this continued well into the nineteenth century.

4

DEATH OF A HIGHWAYMAN

Bramfield, 1782

Travellers along the rutted roads and treacherous forest tracks of eighteenth-century Hertfordshire continually ran the gauntlet of footpads, robbers and highwaymen who terrorised this wooded county. But in the 1780s there had been a spate of particularly violent robberies by an unknown highwayman and his cruel gang which plunged the countryside into great fear. One Mr Kent of Benington was waylaid one evening as he returned home to his farm. A group of men dressed in smock frocks and with blackened faces launched themselves at him from the hedgerows, wielding sticks. The farmer bravely put up resistance, but was overpowered and beaten to death, his body being thrown into his cart where the horse eventually took it home.

On Saturday 28 December 1782, at about midday, a group of men sat drinking in the Farmers' Rooms of the old Maidenhead Inn, Hertford. The topic of discussion was the recent robberies and they speculated who the villains might be. Walking among them was a respectably dressed man wearing a white apron and carrying a basket of pies, cakes and sweets which he was offering for sale. From the familiar manner in which he was addressed he was apparently well known by the farmers, and many partook hungrily of his wares. Soon the conversation turned to the robbery of a few days before when Mr Robert Pellatt had been attacked on his way home by a highwayman who had relieved him of his watch and a sum of money which he had concealed in his boot. It was remarked that it seemed strange the robber knew exactly where Mr Pellatt's valuables were hidden.

Overhearing this conversation were two athletic-looking men, the brothers Whittenbury. Both were around six feet in height and the younger of the two, Robert, was looking very pleased with himself, telling his elder brother Benjamin that he had made the large sum of £200 at the farmers' market that morning. For this information he was chastised by another farmer, who warned that they must all be extra vigilant with the countryside plagued by such a gang of brigands. But the admonishment was laughed off in the good humour of ale, the group feeling assured that there was little likelihood of two such powerfully built men being attacked.

The gun that killed Walter Clibbon, now in Hertford Museum. (Reproduced with permission of Hertford Museum)

At around three in the afternoon, replete with ale and pies, the brothers Whittenbury left the Maidenhead Inn and began to make their way home. Robert had sent his son William on ahead with the cart, he himself preferring to walk with his brother.

As late afternoon approached on that cold December day the countryside through which William had to ride was growing dark. He was passing Oakenvalley Bottom on the Datchworth to Bramfield road, just outside the village of Tewin, when three men with blackened faces rushed out of the woodland, one armed with a gun, the others with sticks. They forced him to stop and searched him and the cart, but finding nothing of value thrashed the horse and made it gallop, causing young William to fall backwards into the cart. As soon as he recovered himself he knew he must warn his father and uncle who would soon be passing along the same way with a large amount of money in their possession. William rode as fast as he could to Queen Hoo Hall, the home of his uncle Benjamin, and called upon his cousins and their farm servant George North for help. Arming themselves with sticks, the young Whittenburys began the journey in haste, a dog at their side. North took down the half-bore flintlock gun from the chimney breast and joined the group.

On their way they met Benjamin who had just parted from his brother, leaving him to walk on alone towards Aston. He turned back with them and they all ran up the hill together, where they found Robert being viciously attacked by the robbers. He was alive, but did not escape without a broken skull. The gang of Whittenburys fell upon the robbers. Benjamin immediately closed with the eldest villain and a vehement fight ensued. Although Benjamin was the bigger of the two, the footpad managed to force him down to the ground and, while kneeling on him, opened a clasp knife and struck at Whittenbury's throat. Benjamin shouted out to North, 'Shoot, Shock, or I am a dead man!' North – nicknamed Shock because of his white hair – immediately pointed the gun and fired at the robber, who, in turning, received the whole charge in the pit of his stomach and fell dead on the ground. At this the robbers took to their heels. One escaped, the other was captured at the foot of the hill. The prisoner was taken to The Horns public house half a mile up the road at Bulls Green to await the arrival of Chief Constable John Carrington, who is still remembered today as a diarist.

The Whittenburys returned with lanterns to the spot where the robber had been shot. It was only then that the identity of the villain who had long been terrorising the district was revealed. The dead man was none other than Walter Clibbon, the affable pieman who had been gossiping with the farmers that very afternoon in the Maidenhead tavern. His body was placed on a hurdle and dragged to The Horns inn where it was deposited in the barn.

On the following day people came for miles around to see for themselves the man who had caused so much fear and anxiety in the county. A rope was fastened to the feet of the corpse and the hurdle dragged around Bulls Green for hours in a macabre carnival fashion, such was the relief and rejoicing at the death of the robber.

Clibbon's body was taken back to the place where he had met his end, at Oakenvalley Bottom, and buried at the roadside with a large wooden post marking the spot as a warning to all. An inscription on the post read: 'Here continues to rot the body of Walter Clibborn [sic], who, with his sons, robbed and ill-treated many persons in this neighbourhood. He was shot near this spot by a farmer's servant while in the act of robbing his master, December 28th, 1782. Please do not deface this.'

Since then there have been many posts, each replaced as the former rots away. During the First World War one post was pulled down and used as a lever to assist an army lorry out of the ditch. It was then tossed to one side and lay buried in the grass for some years before it was replaced in 1927 and the spot once again marked for all to see. The remains of the original wooden post are preserved at Hertford Museum, along with the handle of a clasp knife and a much-corroded razor which were found at the site.

Clibbon's son, who escaped, made his way back to his father's house at Wareside and, after informing his mother of old Clibbon's death and the capture of his nineteen-year-old brother Joseph, left the place and was not

Clibbon's Post, marking the spot where the highwayman lost his life in 1782. (HALS D/EGr/19)

heard of for years after. He was then reputedly recognised at Walthamstow where he was considered 'a quiet, inoffensive man' and followed the occupation of a hedger. No further action was taken against him. After his death, it was revealed that Walter Clibbon had eleven children, the eldest of which were groomed as footpads, and his wife sometimes accompanied him on his robberies.

Mrs Clibbon and her son Joseph were tried. She was acquitted but Joseph was hanged on 7 March 1783 on the gallows on the Stanstead Road at Hertford for the Whittenbury robbery and various other crimes. When the Clibbons' house was searched, a variety of articles were discovered hidden in the thatch, including the watch taken from Mr Pellatt's boot. At last it was understood how the robbers had known this was where he had concealed his valuables – Clibbon would have overheard him mentioning it to friends in one of the inns.

George 'Shock' North was tried for murder but was acquitted and died years later at Watton-at-Stone. The gun which he used to kill Clibbon now also resides in Hertford Museum. Benjamin Whittenbury died in December 1801 and was buried at Tewin.

Clibbon's Post can still be seen today on the woodland verge of the Datchworth to Bramfield road, a grim reminder of the violent events that took place here over 200 years ago.

5

THE NIGHT OF THE DOUBLE MURDER

Hoddesdon, 1807

The crimes of Thomas Simmons one autumn night in 1807 in Hoddesdon were described by a contemporary commentator as 'two of the most atrocious Murders perhaps ever committed'.

According to one pamphlet written shortly after the murders Simmons was born on 26 May 1787, the son of a net maker and charwoman who were both dead by 1807.[†] His appearance was unbecoming. He was described as being 5 feet 6 inches tall with a vacant stare, a long nose and 'the appearance of an ignorant, harmless, country clown'.

Thomas Simmons began working for George Borham around the year 1804. Borham was an aged, infirm, respectable Quaker farmer, who had lived in Hoddesdon for many years (his name appears in the earliest Hoddesdon directory published in the late eighteenth century). There, Simmons courted Borham's servant Elizabeth Harris who was much older than him. Simmons proposed marriage but was turned down, partly because Harris had been advised by her mistress, Ann Borham, not to get too involved with Simmons. Mrs Borham was wary of his 'ferocious and ungovernable temper, which he frequently displayed'. After being turned down by Harris, Simmons beat her and often told her that he would kill her because of her rejection.

It was not just on the domestic front that Simmons's 'ferocious and sanguinary disposition' was causing trouble. The venerable Mr Borham's farm was managed by Joseph Simpson who frequently had to rebuke Simmons for his idleness and negligence. Simmons threatened to kill Simpson as well, saying he would gladly hang for it.

Simmons's aggressive behaviour ultimately led to his dismissal from Borham's employ but he soon found a job at Messrs Christie and Co.'s

---

† There was a Thomas Simmons baptised on 9 July 1786 at Broxbourne church, the son of Luke John Simmons and Sarah Simmons. There were two Sarah Simmons buried in the Broxbourne churchyard in 1787 and Luke John was buried there in 1796, which would have left Thomas an orphan.

Hoddesdon at the end of the eighteenth century. (HALS CV HOD/29)

brewery in Hoddesdon. It was while working here that Simmons learned Elizabeth Harris had begun stepping out with a Mr Dighton. Infuriated, Simmons was often heard to say that he would 'do for them all', and his spleen was particularly directed against Harris and Mrs Borham. On Tuesday 20 October 1807 Simmons was very anxious to leave work as soon as possible.

That night the Borhams were holding a gathering consisting of Mr Borham, his wife Ann and their four daughters, Ann, Elizabeth, Sarah and their married sister Mrs Warner who was visiting. Also present was Sarah Hummerstone,[†] the housekeeper of the Hoddesdon pub the Black Lion inn (now the Salisbury Arms). At around 8.30 p.m. (some accounts give the time as around 9 or 9.15) Elizabeth Harris was in the kitchen when she heard Simmons coming towards the house via the farmyard into an interior court called the stone yard. Simmons was swearing violently and ignored Harris's pleas for him to be quiet.

Harris retreated to the wash house, shutting the door behind her. Simmons struck at her with a knife through the lattice. Mrs Hummerstone heard the

---

[†] Her surname is spelt several ways in different sources. Hummerstone is taken from the Broxbourne burial register.

commotion and came out into the yard to investigate. She saw Simmons and told him to go away but he struck her on the head, knocking off her bonnet. Hummerstone ran back into the house, pursued by Simmons. From the wash house Elizabeth Harris heard shrieks and cries of 'murder'.

Simmons had stabbed Hummerstone in the neck before he burst into the parlour where the Borham family were all congregated except for the younger Ann who was upstairs. Mrs Warner was nearest to Simmons and he mercilessly stabbed her several times in the neck and chest. Warner, who was still seated at the time, fell from her chair and died. Elizabeth and Sarah Borham ran upstairs to join their sister as Simmons turned on Mrs Borham, stabbing her in the neck.

Simmons returned to look for Harris. He found her and she cried out 'murder' then ran into the sitting room where she saw a body on the floor. Simmons chased Harris down the passage where they encountered George Borham with a poker in his hand. Simmons knocked down the aged farmer who was too frail to stop him, caught hold of Harris and threw her down to the ground and drew his knife across her throat. Luckily Harris had managed to put her hand in the way of the blade. She wrestled the knife from Simmons

A contemporary woodcut showing the events at Borham House on the night of the double murder. (St Albans Library)

before he could attempt a second cut. Simmons then fled. Harris ran into the street where her cries of 'murder' alerted the neighbourhood.

A local surgeon, Samuel James, was quickly called. He arrived at the house to find Sarah Hummerstone leaning against some palings near a door, barely alive. She died around three minutes later from a wound in her neck near to her spine. James confirmed that Mrs Warner was dead. Mrs Borham's neck wound was dressed and it proved not to be fatal. Mr Borham was prostrate on the floor with the poker by his side. He suffered from palsy and had been too weak to use the weapon against Simmons.

The search for Thomas Simmons began in earnest. Neighbour George Britton had heard of the murder and hurried to the house. He found Simmons's hat in the cow house. The fugitive, wearing a bloody smock frock, was discovered by Thomas Copperthwaite concealed under straw in a crib some 100 yards from the house. Simmons was taken to the Bell alehouse where he was bound and handcuffed until the next morning when he would appear at a coroner's inquest at the Black Bull pub.

When Benjamin Fairfax of the Black Bull inn went to collect Simmons on Wednesday morning he found him close to death. The ligatures used to bind him were so tight that they had restricted his circulation throughout the night. Fairfax quickly cut the bindings and Simmons recovered in time to appear at the inquest.

The news of the terrible events of the previous night had quickly spread. At that time Hoddesdon was not yet an ecclesiastical parish (and would not become one until 1844) and much of the town was still served by the church at neighbouring Broxbourne. The vicar was the Reverend William Jones, who wrote about the murders in his diary on 21 October. The entry contained the shocking information that Mrs Warner had been heavily pregnant:

Poor, wretched mortals! what horrible consequences follow their being given up into the power of Satan, & their own mad, unbridled passions, for ever so short a season! I know not how even to glance at two most horrid murders, which were last night committed in my parish, at old Mr. Borham, the farmer's house. Mrs. Warner, B——m's daughter, who was within 5 or 6 weeks of her delivery, & Mrs. Hummerstone, Batty's house-keeper, were the poor sufferers. The villain's name is Simmons, not more than 20 years of age! To describe the shocking circumstances would be too painful!

Gracious Heaven! what must have been the state of the poor wretch's mind before, as well as after, the commission of deeds so atrocious! who would not infinitely prefer the sad lot of the pitiable sufferers to that of their murderer, – even were it possible that the laws of his country & the long-suffering of God should not let him linger out his existence to the latest possible period of human life! His very existence must be an intolerable burden to him! And what has he not to dread – here-after!

The inquest was heard before Hertford coroner Benjamin Rooke. It began at 11 a.m. on 21 October and concluded nine hours later. Simmons, still covered in the blood of his victims, expressed his sorrow for his actions and said that he had no previous intention to kill Sarah Hummerstone or any of the Borham family, only Elizabeth Harris. He further denied being involved in two recent unsuccessful attempts to break into Borham's house.

After hearing the evidence the coroner's jury immediately returned a verdict of wilful murder against Thomas Simmons, who was taken to Hertford Gaol to await trial at the next Hertford Assizes. On the way there he told the constable escorting him an extraordinary tale. Simmons said that at the moment he was going to strike Elizabeth Harris a second time:

> he heard an odd kind of fluttering noise behind him, and on looking back, saw a brown figure, with wings extended, which frightened him so much, that he let the maid take the knife out of his hand, and crawled out of the back-door, on his hands and knees, and the figure followed him to the garden gate; that he then saw no more of it, and fled to a cow-shed, some way off, and covered himself over with straw, where he lay until he was taken.

The bodies of Sarah Hummerstone and Mrs Warner remained at Borham House until their interment. On 3 November funeral services for the pair were preached at the chapel in Hoddesdon. The chapel was full by 2.30 p.m., half an hour before the service commenced. The Reverend Mr Bush addressed the congregation on the 'fickle tenure of human life, exemplified in the event before them', and said that a Christian life best prepared the way to death. Sarah Hummerstone was buried in the churchyard at Broxbourne. Alongside her entry in the burial register the Reverend Mr Jones added the mournful addendum 'murdered by Simmons'.

Back in Hertford Gaol Simmons, shackled in 25 lb of chains, was behaving in a quiet manner while awaiting his trial, although one newspaper reported that he was 'raving mad' and had refused food for days. Another hoped that the 'melancholy catastrophe will operate as a caution to masters and mistresses of families, to be very circumspect in admitting followers after their servants, either by the name of sweethearts or acquaintances'.

When he entered the gaol Simmons could not even recite the Lord's Prayer but later learned several others by heart. He received a visit from the Reverend Mr Jones, to whom he said that he was sorry for what he had done and cried. According to a contemporary pamphlet, *Fairburn's Edition of the Trial of Thomas Simmons*, Simmons shared a cell with a deer stealer named Thomas Champion who read prayers to Simmons during the day and prayed with him at night. This may have been Thomas Champion of Totteridge who was tried at the same Assize as Simmons for attempting to kill, wound and destroy a fallow deer. Champion was found guilty and sentenced to death but this was

From a correct likeness
Drawn from the life
by Mr Angelo.

THOMAS SIMMONS.

The horrid and inhuman Murderer of Mrs Hummerstone, and Mrs Warner at the house of
Mr Boreham a Quaker at Hoddesdon. in Hertfordshire. on Tuesday Evening. October the 20. 1807.

Etched and Pub. by T. Rowlandson Nov. g. 1807. N. 1 James St. Adelphi

Thomas Simmons at Hertford Gaol awaiting his trial for murder. (HALS D/EX 877/1)

30

commuted to seven years' transportation to an Australian penal colony.

Thomas Simmons stood trial only for the murder of Sarah Hummerstone. Because Mrs Warner and her family had been Quakers, they would not prosecute Simmons for her murder. At this time the majority of prosecutions were brought by private individuals on behalf of the victims of crime or the victims themselves. A Mr W. White, Benjamin Fairfax of the Black Bull inn and churchwarden Mr M.J. Brown financed the prosecution of Simmons.

The trial took place on 4 March 1808 before Mr Justice Heath at Hertford. Simmons was indicted on the charge of murder:

> not having the fear of God before his eyes, but being moved and seduced by the instigation of the Devil, upon Sarah Hommerston, feloniously, wilfully, and with malice aforethought, did make an assault, and that he the said Thomas Simmons, with a certain knife, which he then and there held in his right hand, wilfully and maliciously did strike and stab the said Sarah Hommerston, in and upon the neck, thereby giving unto her one mortal wound, of which she died.

The court was crowded as the prosecution called their witnesses to tell the story of the events at Mr Borham's house on 20 October. Elizabeth Harris was in a state of great agitation and had to be supported while she gave her evidence. Benjamin Rooke was called to give evidence. The report of the inquest stated that Simmons's 'sole design was against Elizabeth Harris'. Rooke apparently told the court that Simmons had said 'he did not intend to have murdered Mrs. Homerston, but he went with an intention of murdering Mrs. Borham, Mrs. Warner, and Elizabeth Harris, the maid servant'. When Simmons was asked if he had anything to say he 'answered in a *careless tone* No!'

Judge Heath told the jury that the case was clear and it was unnecessary for him to address any points to them. Simmons had confessed his guilt more than once. The jury found Simmons guilty of the murder of Sarah Hummerstone and the judge decreed that he would hang the next Monday and his body be anatomised. Simmons 'heard the sentence of death with great indifference, and walked coolly from the Bar' to meet his maker.

POSTSCRIPT

Nine days after the double murder George Borham wrote his last will and testament. It was proved in London in January 1808, which means George Borham did not live long enough to witness Thomas Simmons's execution.

Not long after the trial of Thomas Simmons the Reverend Mr Jones of Broxbourne fell ill and ordered a coffin to be made for him. He recovered and moved the coffin to his study, fixed shelves in it and used it as a bookcase until his death in 1821.

Borham House was demolished in 1965.

6

THE SENSATIONAL CRIME OF REGENCY ENGLAND

Aldenham, 1823

It was in the smoky gambling halls and boxing rings of Regency London that three men's paths were to cross and the names of John Thurtell, Joseph Hunt and William Probert were propelled into national notoriety.

The brutal murder of William Weare at Aldenham in 1823 presented little mystery and the circumstances inspired scant compassion for the victim, yet the case became the most notorious in the country. The main reason was that this

A gaming room such as that in which John Thurtell, Joseph Hunt and William Probert would meet.

was the first trial by newspaper where the press, sparing no detail to satisfy the British fascination with murder, virtually condemned the prisoners before the trial even began. Labelled 'the most literary murder', the events of the night of 24 October 1823 appeared not only in the rapidly growing popular press, but in theatres, novels, books and broadsheets. It was also the first time the press came into serious conflict with the courts over their handling of the proceedings.

William Weare, an ex-waiter from the Globe Tavern in Fleet Street, was a professional gambler and a member of a gang of villains of the Regency prizefighting, card playing, horseracing, cockfighting and brawling set known as the 'Fancy'. He had a long-term mistrust of banks, so carried cash on his person, sometimes up to £2,000, in an old pocket book which he placed beneath his shirt, next to his skin. All was going well until he fell foul of a fellow gambler sharing the unsavoury underworld of nineteenth-century organised crime.

John Thurtell, born 21 December 1794 in Norwich, had joined the Navy at fourteen and achieved the rank of second lieutenant. He resigned in 1814 and his father set him up in a fabric business which collapsed seven years later. He was then lured to London and got heavily involved in pugilism and, with his girlfriend Mary Dodson, took on the Black Boy pub in Long Acre. Prizefighting and gambling became his life, but they left Thurtell with some heavy debts. In January 1823 he appeared in front of Mr Justice Park trying to claim insurance for a fire in his fabric warehouse. The judge reprimanded him, 'You are in the lowest state of degradation in point of moral feeling' – an important observation as this would not be the last time Thurtell and the judge were to meet.

Of the two men who were to become Thurtell's accomplices in crime, William Probert, born in 1789, was a former London wine merchant and another bankrupt. He was subsequently imprisoned, once for debt and then for theft. He took a lease on a small farmhouse in Gills Hill Lane, Aldenham and was rumoured to be operating an

From top: John Thurtell, William Probert, Joseph Hunt.

Thurtell pulled out a penknife and cut Weare's throat ...

... to make sure his victim was dead he pulled the trigger once ...

... the body was dragged into a ditch ...

illegal distillery. Both he and Thurtell frequented the Army and Navy tavern in London, which was under the management of Joseph Hunt, born in 1797. Hunt had also been imprisoned for debt and was described as a 'good natured fool'. He was a good singer and this talent he would find useful as an alibi for his involvement in the forthcoming murder.

The victim had cheated Thurtell at a game of cards, leaving him with a £300 debt and making him a laughing stock in the London gambling circuit. On Friday 24 October 1823 Thurtell invited Weare to Hertfordshire for some shooting on his friend Probert's farm. They rode in a horse gig along the Edgware Road. Probert and Hunt were close behind but spent too long dallying at inns along the route so arrived too late to take part in the murder. The road soon became a quiet country lane and Thurtell lashed the horse harshly. As they turned into the dark labyrinth of Gills Hill Lane, Thurtell swung on Weare and fired a pistol but it was faulty and only grazed his cheekbone. Weare leapt from the gig, shouting that he would repay the £300 if his life was spared, but he was overpowered by Thurtell and thrown to the ground. A fierce struggle ensued.

Thurtell pulled out a penknife, cut Weare's throat and smashed him over the head with the butt of the pistol. Then, just to make sure his victim was dead, Thurtell once again pulled the trigger and shot Weare for a second time.

. . . the three returned to the murder scene to retrieve the body . . .

Thurtell rifled the body and dragged it into a ditch, but in the darkness lost the pistol and knife. He rode back to meet the others at Probert's cottage. The money was shared out and the three went back to the murder scene to retrieve the body. The corpse was bundled into a sack, weighted down and thrown into a pond on Probert's land, but was later removed to another pond three miles away at Hill's Slough.

. . . the corpse was first thrown into the pond near Probert's home, Gill's Hill Cottage. . . .

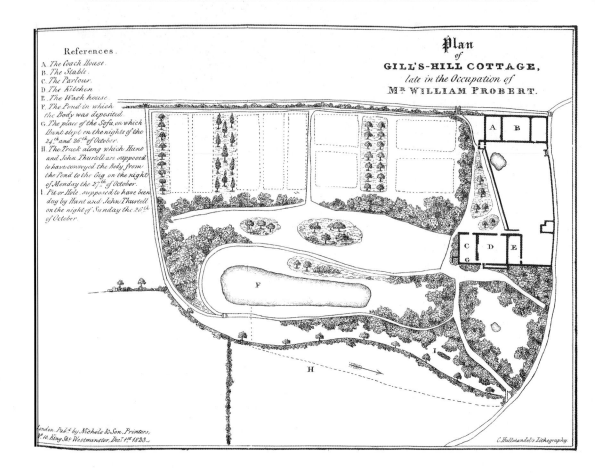

Plan
of
GILL'S-HILL COTTAGE,
late in the Occupation of
Mr WILLIAM PROBERT.

References.

A. The Coach House.
B. The Stable.
C. The Parlour.
D. The Kitchen.
E. The Wash house.
F. The Pond in which
the Body was deposited.
G. The place of the Sofa on which
Hunt slept on the nights of the
24th and 26th of October.
H. The Track along which Hunt
and John Thurtell are supposed
to have conveyed the Body from
the Pond to the Gig on the night
of Monday the 27th of October.
I. Pit or Hole supposed to have been
dug by Hunt and John Thurtell
on the night of Sunday the 26th
of October.

London. Publd. by Nichols & Son, Printers,
No 10. King St. Westminster, Decr. 1st 1823.

C. Hullmandel's Lithography.

Robert Clutterbuck. (HALS Acc 3877)

At daybreak the following morning Thurtell and Hunt went back to the lane and tried unsuccessfully to locate the murder weapons. They were spotted searching furtively in the hedgerows by two workmen, ironically repairing the road for the first time in forty years. The gun with bits of hair and brain attached to the butt and the bloodstained knife were eventually retrieved by the workmen, who handed them over to their supervisor, farmer Charles Nicholls, Probert's nearest neighbour.

Nicholls reported the discovery to the Watford magistrates at their petty sessions when they sat on Tuesday 28 October. A thorough investigation then ensued, led primarily by county historian Robert Clutterbuck (1772–1831), who requested the assistance of the Bow Street Runners from London.

Hunt was forced to reveal the location of Weare's body.

Many witnesses were examined throughout the day and proceedings continued throughout the night until 3 a.m. the following morning, when enough circumstantial evidence had been gathered to justify the arrest of Thurtell, Hunt and Probert, despite the lack of a body. Friends of Weare, knowing of his weekend plans with Thurtell, had already reported him missing and suspicion was gathering that he was the likely victim of the supposed murder.

The magistrates pressured Hunt to make a confession, promising he would not hang. Duly, Hunt revealed the location of Weare's body, concocting a preposterous story that he was innocent, and was at the cottage merely because he had been paid to sing, not to be an accessory to murder. Weare's body was exhumed from its watery grave on Thursday 30 October.

Following the coroner's inquest at the Artichoke Inn on 31 October Weare was ignominiously buried on a stormy night at 11 p.m. on 1 November, next to the grave of Martha Ray, an earlier murder victim, in Elstree churchyard.

Weare was buried on a stormy night in Elstree churchyard.

Calendar of the Prisoners,

IN THE GAOL OF THE SAID COUNTY, FOR TRIAL,

AT THE GAOL DELIVERY,

HERTFORD,

ON THURSDAY THE 4th. DAY OF DECEMBER, 1823,

Before Mr. Justice Parke, & Mr. Justice Holroyd.

No.	Name.	Age.

14—JOHN THURTELL, ...30,—*Silk Merchant, . . Norwich, ...* Committed 30th. October, 1823, by Robert Clutterbuck, Esq. charged on the oaths of Philip Smith, and others, with wilfully and feloniously murdering William Weare, late of Lyon's Inn, in the county of Middlesex, Gent. by shooting him with a certain loaded pistol. The said John Thurtell is also detained by virtue of a Warrant of Benjamin Rooke, Gent. Coroner of the said county of Hertford, charged on oath, with the wilful murder of the said William Weare.

15—JOSEPH HUNT, ...26,—*Gent. . King's-Street, . . Golden Square, . .* Committed 1st. November,
16—WILLIAM PROBERT, .33,—*Wine Merchant, . . Elstree, . . . Herts. . . .* 1823, by Benjamin Rooke, Gent. Coroner of the said county of Hertford, charged on oath, with being accessaries before the fact to the wilful Murder of William Weare.

(Hals DIEX 954/3/1)

The trial opened on 4 December 1823 at the Hertford Assizes under Mr Justice Park, who now encountered Thurtell for a second time. Thurtell's lawyer complained it was a 'trial by newspaper' because the press had reported some highly defamatory stories about his client. The judge agreed, adding that because of this the accused knew all that would be produced against him at his trial. The trial was postponed until the following month.

Tuesday 6 January saw the reopening of this long-awaited trial. The evening before, the road from London to Hertford had been jam-packed with carriages and every inn was full. As early as 4 a.m. on the Tuesday the street leading from the court house to the gaol was filled with crowded vehicles. The judge had difficulty getting in, which did little to improve his mood.

Thurtell remained resolute to the end, making a dramatic speech protesting his innocence, but to no avail as he and Hunt received the death sentence. Hunt was reprieved and transported to Australia on 16 March 1824 where he eventually became constable of Bathurst, New South Wales. Probert, who also turned King's evidence, was released, but was despised and treated with contempt for his actions. On 20 June 1825 he was hanged for the crime of horse stealing and his widow later committed suicide.

The long-awaited trial reopened on Tuesday 6 January . . .

. . . Thurtell was resolute to the end, Hunt was reprieved and transported to Australia, Probert turned King's evidence.

Thurtell was executed at Hertford on 9 January 1824 on a modern drop gallows. An estimated 15,000 people attended in support of Thurtell, who was much admired for his courage and whose bravery on the scaffold endeared him to the 'Fancy'. Mr Willson, keeper of Hertford Gaol, sent a bill to the magistrates for his extra expenses in maintaining security and for replacing his cart shed and pigsty, which had been destroyed in the fray.

AN EXACT REPRESENTATION OF JOHN THURTELL.

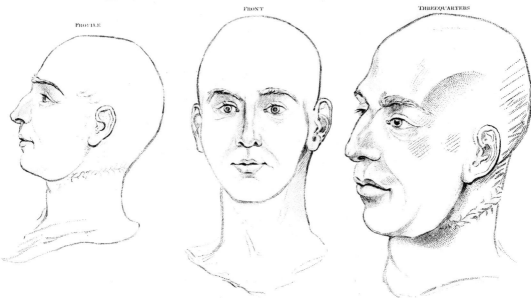

As he appeared in St. Bartholomew's Hospital being the only exact Likenesses taken of him after his Execution.

Thurtell's body was left suspended for an hour before being taken into the care of Mr Colbeck, a surgeon. In the evening a gentleman from the Phrenological Society was allowed to take a cast from the back of the deceased's head and subsequent drawings were said to promise a 'faithful representation' of the villain.

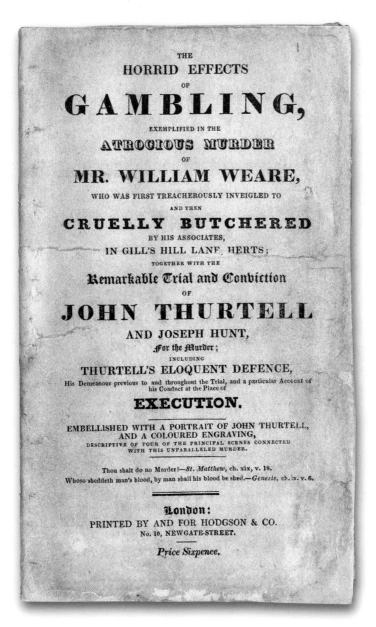

THE
HORRID EFFECTS
OF
GAMBLING,
EXEMPLIFIED IN THE
ATROCIOUS MURDER
OF
MR. WILLIAM WEARE,
WHO WAS FIRST TREACHEROUSLY INVEIGLED TO
AND THEN
CRUELLY BUTCHERED
BY HIS ASSOCIATES,
IN GILL'S HILL LANE, HERTS;
TOGETHER WITH THE
Remarkable Trial and Conviction
OF
JOHN THURTELL
AND JOSEPH HUNT,
For the Murder;
INCLUDING
THURTELL'S ELOQUENT DEFENCE,
His Demeanour previous to and throughout the Trial, and a particular Account of
his Conduct at the Place of
EXECUTION.

EMBELLISHED WITH A PORTRAIT OF JOHN THURTELL,
AND A COLOURED ENGRAVING,
DESCRIPTIVE OF FOUR OF THE PRINCIPAL SCENES CONNECTED
WITH THIS UNPARALLELED MURDER.

Thou shalt do no Murder!—*St. Matthew*, ch. xix, v. 18.
Whoso sheddeth man's blood, by man shall his blood be shed.—*Genesis*, ch. ix. v. 6.

London:
PRINTED BY AND FOR HODGSON & CO.
No. 10, NEWGATE-STREET.

Price Sixpence.

This murder, more than any before it, inspired many writers and a whole library of books, pamphlets, articles and broadsheets was produced. This is just one of them. (HALS)

Entry in the diary of Thomas Newcome, Rector of Shenley (1822–49). It reads: 'August 17. I was shewn a piece of Thurtells tanned skin by the Justice Clerk at Watford petty Sessions!' (HALS Acc 2800)

Perhaps Thurtell's life might have turned out differently had it not been for the malign influence of the 'Fancy'. Even the judge had been moved by the courage with which he bore his sentence, saying:

It cannot but give great compunction to every feeling mind that a person, who, from this conduct this day, had shown that he was born with capacity for better things – who, according to his statement, received in his childhood, religious impressions from a kind and careful mother, who in his youth served his country without reproach, should, notwith-standing, have been guilty of so foul and a detestable crime.

7

A TRIPLE HANGING

The murder of William Bennett began as a robbery of an army pensioner by four ruffians in the parish of Tewin, a small rural village some three miles from the county town of Hertford. After the capture of the murderers an extraordinary chain of events unfolded, resulting in the intervention of the prime minister and three executions.

On 25 October 1837 four unemployed local labourers, George Fletcher, William Roach, David Sams and Thomas Taylor, were in the Cold Bath public house in Hertford. William Bennett, a 59-year-old army pensioner from Burnham Green in Tewin, later entered the Cold Bath after collecting his quarterly army pension of £8 0s 3d from another Hertford inn.

The labourers were seen asking Bennett if he had collected his pension before they left the Cold Bath shortly after 4 p.m. Bennett left five to ten minutes later and made his way towards Tewin, as did the labourers. Three of the labourers were later seen entering Scrubb's Wood in Tewin and at about 6 p.m. three men were spotted running from the wood towards Hertford.

Bennett failed to return home that night and his body was discovered lying in a shallow rut in Scrubb's Field in Tewin early the next morning. At the coroner's inquest held that afternoon a team of surgeons concluded that Bennett had died by violent means. His body was extensively bruised about the face and head, and death had been caused by ruptured blood vessels exerting a fatal pressure upon the brain. A verdict of wilful murder by some person or persons unknown was returned.

From descriptions given of the labourers by eyewitnesses, Fletcher, Roach, Taylor and Sams immediately came under suspicion. Fletcher and Sams were arrested on 27 October. Roach was arrested in London on 9 November. Taylor could not be found at this time and remained a fugitive for another year.

Fletcher, Roach and Sams were held separately in Hertford Gaol where they all made confessions which heavily implicated Thomas Taylor in Bennett's murder. The confessions were made independently so that none of the men were influenced by what the others had said, nor did they know that their fellow prisoners had confessed. Despite the fact that the statements were made by men who were soon to go on trial for murder, knowing that their

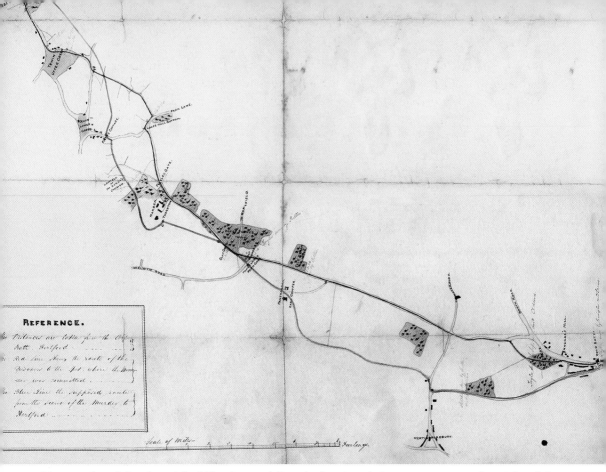

Map produced for the trial of Fletcher and Roach showing their movements on the night of George Bennett's murder. (HALS D/P 106/10/2)

lives may depend on them, they proved to be of vital importance and were the sole accounts of the murder of William Bennett.

Sams was the first to confess. By his account, Roach had initially suggested that they rob Bennett. He added that Roach had approached Bennett in the Cold Bath and asked if he had collected his pension. Sams had not been present when the attack took place for he was well known in Tewin where his father lived and feared being recognised. He also knew Bennett. Sams stayed behind when his companions entered Scrubb's Wood in search of Bennett.

Sams said Fletcher, Roach and Taylor returned to him but they did not tell him that they had killed Bennett, although Roach said he had kicked Bennett in the side of the head two or three times. Sams added that Taylor had told him, 'I kicked him once by the side of the head.' This confession was the only one of the three that did not implicate Taylor more heavily than Fletcher and Roach in the assault.

Roach's confession soon followed. He accused Taylor of declaring that he and his companions would get Bennett's money. Roach then blamed Fletcher for initiating the attack on Bennett by running up to the pensioner and throwing him to the ground. Having robbed Bennett, he and Roach ran off. Roach then stated that Bennett was still alive for he was getting up when Taylor kicked him, 'but whether once or twice, I cannot say'. Roach further damned Taylor by stating that Taylor said that, 'he had given him such a —— [*sic*] kick under the ear, that he knew he would be quiet for some time.' Roach vehemently denied kicking Bennett when he discovered that Sams had accused him of saying he had done so.

Fletcher was the last to confess. He accused Sams of inciting the robbery. Fletcher substantiated Roach's confession by admitting that he had initiated the assault on Bennett by pulling the pensioner to the ground, and confirmed that Bennett was alive when he and Roach ran off. He added that he saw Taylor beat Bennett with his fist. Fletcher thought that Bennett was still alive and feared he would raise the alarm when he got home. Taylor said, 'He will send nobody after us yet, for I have stunned him.' Taylor then told Fletcher that he had kicked Bennett either on the head or ear. Fletcher also said that after he and Roach had run off they had to wait for Taylor to catch up with them. This might have given the impression that Taylor had stayed behind to continue assaulting Bennett. However, there was an alternative explanation for Taylor's delay in leaving the scene of the attack; he had a sprained ankle.

There was obviously no confession from the fugitive Taylor. After the murder of Bennett he had gone to Hoddesdon where he had met an acquaintance, Charles Banks. The news of Bennett's death had already reached Hoddesdon. According to Banks, Taylor admitted to him that he had been involved in the attack on Bennett and that all four of them had agreed to rob Bennett but he, Fletcher and Sams became indecisive and almost changed their minds. Roach had urged them on and the robbery went ahead. Taylor said that 'one of them' had knocked Bennett down but he got up and told his attackers that he knew them. Taylor claimed to have run off and knew nothing of what happened afterwards.

The coroner's inquest and post-mortem on Bennett had been unable to establish whether Taylor had actually struck the fatal blow. Bennett's death was ascribed to 'divers mortal bruises and contusions upon the head'. Consequently Fletcher, Roach and Taylor were all indicted for the murder of William Bennett. Sams faced a charge of inciting Fletcher, Roach and Taylor to commit the deed.

The confessions made an immediate impression. Crucially Fletcher, Roach and Sams's confessions were all believed. The Town Clerk of Hertford took a separate set of statements from the men and in his opinion 'it was evident from the manner in which they coincided in every important particular, that the prisoners were telling the truth'. Doubts were raised over the possible outcome of their trial for murder. Before their trial at the Hertfordshire Lent Assizes of 1838 the Clerk of the Assizes recommended that an additional indictment be prepared against Fletcher and Roach for highway robbery, 'in the event of their being acquitted for murder'.

Judge Sir John Vaughan warned the jury to be wary of the confessions of Fletcher, Roach and Sams, for it was from these confessions that they would have to decide the guilt or innocence of the prisoners. Despite their not guilty pleas Fletcher and Roach were found guilty of the murder of William Bennett, as their (and Taylor's) assault on Bennett had clearly resulted in his death. Sams was acquitted after the judge told the jury that the charge against him was very weak. This was a fair point as only Fletcher had blamed Sams for suggesting the robbery. Whereas in previous years a felon convicted of murder was executed within forty-eight hours of being sentenced to death, Fletcher and Roach now had a period of twelve days to appeal. This was because 'according to custom at Hertford' at least two Sundays had to intervene between the date of sentencing and the date of execution. The date of sentencing had been Friday 2 March and the date of execution had been set for 14 March.

A growing national opposition to the death penalty at this time, along with unsuccessful attempts to abolish it altogether, had resulted in the number of offences punishable by death being significantly reduced. Attempts were swiftly made to attempt to prevent the executions of Fletcher and Roach, most significantly through local support of a petition appealing for mercy and a commutation of their death sentences. It bore the supporting signatures of seventy-four of the most prominent residents of Hertford and the surrounding parishes of Tewin, Bengeo and Hertingfordbury.

A significant proportion of the seventy-four signees (all men) stated their positions and occupations, which revealed that many had been personally involved in the investigation into Bennett's death and the prosecution and trial of Fletcher and Roach. These included the foreman of the jury, a surgeon who performed the autopsy on Bennett, the solicitor who recorded the confessions, the chaplain of Hertford Gaol and the solicitor for the prosecution. The clergy was also well represented by curates and churchwardens and a dissenting (nonconformist) minister. Numerous prominent Hertford officials added their names to the list. These included the mayor, the alderman, two justices of the peace, a councillor and a deputy clerk of the peace. The remainder consisted of local tradesmen, artisans, gentlemen and schoolmasters.

Fletcher and Roach did not write their petition. Both were illiterate and had to sign the document with a cross. The petition was carefully worded and clearly written on parchment, suggesting that someone familiar with compiling legal documents had drawn it up. It is possible that Fletcher and Roach's case elicited a sufficient degree of local support to raise enough funds to pay for the petition, or possibly to persuade a local lawyer to provide his services free of charge. The explanation for the level of support Fletcher and

Roach received was owing to the popular belief that Taylor had struck the fatal blow and was therefore the murderer, along with a genuine desire not to see any more executions in Hertfordshire.

The petition expressed Fletcher and Roach's willingness to accept any alternative punishment should their sentences be commuted. If reprieved, the likeliest punishment would have been transportation overseas. This method of punishment removed the offenders from the country to penal colonies in Australia if their offence was not deemed serious enough to warrant a death penalty, but too serious for a lesser punishment. Fletcher and Roach laid out their arguments for obtaining mercy:

· Their lack of early parental control: 'your petitioners have not been fostered by parental care'.

· Their lack of education: 'nor have been endowed with the advantages of the commonest rudiments of education. . . . they cannot either of them read or write'. (This was hardly exceptional though. The vast majority of prisoners in English prisons at this time were either illiterate or semi-literate.)

· Their youth. Fletcher was twenty-one, Roach was eighteen (nor was this a particularly persuasive argument, as many people executed were under twenty-one years old).

It was not until the end of their representation that what would prove to be their strongest ground for mercy was raised – they had only intended to rob Bennett. The murder had not been their 'thought or intention'. Furthermore, Fletcher and Roach said that they had not armed themselves or used any weapons in the attack on Bennett.

It was never doubted that they had not intended to kill Bennett but the lack of a weapon was a contentious issue. At a magistrates' examination of Fletcher, Roach and Sams held in November 1837 surgeon John Davies, who had examined Bennett's body, testified that Bennett's head wounds could have been inflicted by 'a short smooth bludgeon, or some instrument of that description'. At the Assizes Davies changed his opinion as to the cause of the wounds. They might have been the result of 'a kick or kicks from the shoes of labouring men'.

Strangely Fletcher and Roach neglected to put forward an argument that Taylor had been more responsible for Bennett's death than they were, as their confessions had implied. Many people familiar with the case believed this to be true because Fletcher and Roach had been quick to point out that they had both seen Taylor strike Bennett when he was still alive. The supporters of this belief might not have known of the medical evidence that suggested Bennett

William Lamb, Lord Melbourne of Brocket Hall, Lemsford. Melbourne was prime minister in 1838 and rejected Fletcher and Roach's petition for mercy. (HALS D/ELb/F109)

had received a much more severe assault than Taylor appeared to have inflicted. Possibly the reason why Fletcher and Roach did not put more blame on to Taylor in their petition was because they themselves knew that this was not wholly true.

Another argument missing from Fletcher and Roach's petition was one regarding their character. If they could prove themselves to be of good character it could have been the best way of persuading a judge to recommend a reprieve, but Fletcher and Roach could not have made such a claim. It emerged after their trial that they admitted to the governor of Hertford Gaol they had previously taken part in several highway robberies with David Sams.

After all the signatures had been collected the petition was handed to the High Sheriff of Hertford, who then forwarded it to the Home Office. Fletcher and Roach's supporters were optimistic about the chances of the petition's success but the prisoners 'did not appear to be buoyed up with any false hopes'.

The fate of Fletcher and Roach was ultimately placed in the hands of Prime Minister Lord Melbourne rather than the Home Secretary who usually dealt with petitions. Coincidentally, Melbourne's family home was Brocket Hall in Lemsford, only a few miles away from Tewin where the murder of Bennett had taken place. Melbourne had served as Home Secretary between 1830 and 1834 so was familiar with the appeal process, and a subsequent examination of the appeal by the Home Secretary Lord John Russell showed that he entirely agreed with Melbourne's assessment of the case.

Lord Melbourne noted the large number of signatures on the petition and the diversity of those people who had signed it. This demonstrated to him that 'it expresses a real feeling & opinion', and was therefore 'deserving of great attention'. From the beginning of his report Melbourne expressed misgivings over granting Fletcher and Roach a reprieve. He could not find any evidence that would lead him to the conclusion that Taylor was more involved in the attack than Fletcher and Roach. The coroner's inquest papers reinforced this fact. The inquest took place the day after the murder of Bennett, before anyone had been caught and charged with the crime, and it concluded that Bennett had been beaten and struck numerous times.

To support this point, Melbourne quoted from the confession of David Sams, 'that he (Roach) had to kick him two or *three times on the head*, & Taylor said, I kicked him once on the side of the head'. Melbourne's assertion had supporting evidence from surgeon John Davies. Davies was quoted as saying that Bennett's corpse displayed eight or nine marks of violence, clearly more than four kicks and a fall could reasonably be expected to produce.

Another point against Fletcher and Roach was that Melbourne seemed to be influenced by the fact that they had confessed to being the most active in the robbery. Melbourne accepted the argument put forward in the petition that Fletcher and Roach had only intended to rob Bennett. He considered it to be the only believable point in the case, and 'it is the point upon which the petitioners rely'. But it was not enough for, as Melbourne concluded, even if Bennett had not died as a result of the attack but had 'been left senseless and incapable of firing the alarm, which, I apprehend, to have been the intention of the prisoners, it would still have been a capital offence'.

Melbourne was quite correct and this point sealed the fate of Fletcher and Roach. In 1837 the Robbery From the Person Act repealed the death penalty for that crime. However, if the robbery was accompanied by serious violence, and there was no avoiding that had happened when Bennett was robbed, then the crime was still a capital one. Melbourne concluded, 'in my opinion the law ought to have taken its course'.

Lord Russell agreed that Melbourne's decision rested upon the law 'which punishes with death robbery accompanied by violence'. Even though Russell felt that if Fletcher and Roach had been charged with robbery with violence, instead of murder, the judge might not have passed a capital sentence, his report reinforced Melbourne's view that this statute should be enforced 'in very aggravated cases of robbery'.

Russell agreed that it was impossible to tell who had been the most responsible for Bennett's death. Fletcher and Roach would 'of course charge the one who has escaped', adding that if Taylor had been caught and tried along with Fletcher and Roach the verdict on the petition would have been the same. Even if Taylor would have made a confession which admitted that he struck the blow that killed Bennett it would not have meant that Fletcher and Roach 'deserve less than a capital punishment'.

The day after their petition was turned down, Fletcher and Roach were hanged outside Hertford Gaol before a crowd of around 4,000 onlookers. One member of the crowd at least had a modicum of sympathy for Fletcher and cried out, 'Fletcher, I hope the Lord will have mercy on you.' Roach addressed the crowd, saying 'I thank the blessed Lord, I am innocent of the murder for which I am suffering.' This declaration, according to one newspaper, had a great effect on the crowd and Roach's assertion was believed.

By the time Fletcher and Roach were executed the idea that the missing Taylor was responsible for Bennett's death was firmly established. Taylor's antecedents were common knowledge which blackened his reputation even further. Details of his previous convictions had been printed in newspapers before the trial of Fletcher and Roach. He had been sentenced to six months' hard labour and whipped for larceny at Hertford in 1837. He had also served time at Chelmsford Gaol for the theft of geese and had been released just three weeks before the attack on Bennett.

Taylor was eventually caught in September 1838 after the police intercepted letters he had written to his mother. He had enlisted in the army at Huntingdon under a false name five days after the attack on Bennett and been sent to Ireland for training. Taylor made a confession accusing Sams of proposing the robbery of Bennett. He declared that he (Taylor) had held Bennett's hands while Fletcher and Roach emptied his pockets and he only began to beat Bennett so that he would let go of Roach. Taylor admitted that as they were leaving Bennett, he attempted to rise. Taylor then kicked him but claimed not to know if his kick landed on Bennett's head or body.

Taylor pleaded not guilty to the murder of William Bennett at the Hertfordshire Lent Assizes of 1839. When David Sams was recalled to give evidence the jury was warned that although Sams was a legitimate witness he had a 'damaged character', and his evidence should be ignored if it was unsupported by other evidence. Sams's 'damaged character' was the result not only of his involvement in the Bennett case, but previous convictions in 1835 and 1837 for offences against the game laws. He was also serving two months for larceny at Hertford Gaol when Taylor was delivered there. Sams would eventually be transported for life for larceny in 1841.

The jury deliberated for a mere fifteen minutes before finding Taylor guilty of murder. When the jury went out to consider their verdict on Fletcher and

Whitehall
13 March 1838

Sir

     I am directed by Lord John Russell to inform you, that having considered the Report of the Judge, Mr Justice Vaughan, who tried the prisoners George Fletcher and William Roach, on whose behalf a Petition for mercy has been received, his Lordship is of opinion, that the Crime of which they have been Convicted is so great, and their guilt so clearly proved, he ought not to recommend the prisoners as objects for the Royal Mercy.—

     I am
Sir
Your most Obedient
humble Servant

S M Phillipps.

J M Carter Esq
&c   &c   &c

The letter from the Home Office informing Hertford magistrate John Carter that Fletcher and Roach's appeal had failed. It was written just one day before their executions. (HALS SH2/4/1/19)

Roach they took several hours to reach the same verdict. The judge, like so many others, had reached the conclusion 'that the prisoner was perhaps the most guilty of all, having given several kicks to the head of the old man'. This was at odds with Judge Vaughan's verdict in the Fletcher and Roach case. It also contradicted Lord Melbourne and John Russell's conclusions with regard to the degree of involvement of Fletcher, Roach and Taylor in Bennett's death.

It appeared that Taylor's kick might have killed Bennett (who was still alive when Taylor inflicted it), but the beating Bennett had already received could have been a major contributory factor to his death and there was no way of knowing if Bennett would have died as a result of the attack even if Taylor had not participated in it.

The prevailing sentiment was that if Fletcher and Roach had hanged for the crime then Taylor must hang too. As one newspaper wrote, 'it was felt it would not be just that the principal offender should escape from the punishment awarded to his companions'.

Taylor did not attempt to earn himself a reprieve by petitioning for he appeared to have given up hope after his death sentence had been passed. Nor was there any evidence that anyone attempted to petition on his behalf. If he had done so it would surely have had even less chance of succeeding than Fletcher and Roach's. Melbourne was still prime minister and Russell was still Home Secretary and their reasons for turning down Fletcher and Roach's petition would have been equally valid for Taylor.

Taylor was executed outside Hertford Gaol on 13 March 1839 before a crowd of between two and three thousand. The crowd displayed no signs of being moved by the event, or having any sympathy for Taylor. After the executions of Fletcher and Roach the diarist William Lucas recorded that Fletcher and Roach were 'Two poor fellows'. A later diary entry regarding Thomas Taylor described him as 'The man principally concerned in the Tewin murder'. The crowd showed even less decorum than at Fletcher and Roach's execution, for 'the day was a carnival to the dissolute of the neighbourhood'. It would be nearly four decades before there was another execution in Hertfordshire.

8

DEATH IN THE LINE OF DUTY

Stevenage, 1857 and Benington, 1871

Mutilated by a thieving labourer, murdered by a poacher and shot by a vicar; by all accounts, a policeman's lot in Victorian Hertfordshire was an extremely hazardous one.

In the early hours of New Year's Day 1844 PC Cornelius Wintle was shot several times by a man of the cloth while on duty in Childwickbury between St Albans and Harpenden.

PC Wintle had been patrolling the area of Childwick Green sometime around 1.20 a.m. when he heard the sound of gunshots behind him coming from the direction of the Reverend Mr Brogden's house. Fearing an attack on the vicarage, the young police constable turned and ran back to the house where, only yards from the outer gate, he received several rounds from the clergyman's shotgun. Wintle fell to the ground, moaning in pain and calling out that he had been shot.

The Reverend Mr Brogden rushed outside with his butler and was horrified to discover the injured person was not an intruder but an officer of the law. Together they attempted to carry him inside, but Wintle insisted he would walk, hoping it would 'circulate the blood a little'. Brogden immediately despatched a servant on horseback to St Albans, some five miles away, to fetch Mr Clarke, the surgeon, who finally arrived at about 3 a.m. Examining Wintle, Clarke pronounced the case serious but with no immediate danger, and the patient was transferred to West Herts Infirmary at Hemel Hempstead.

Superintendent Pye of the Hertfordshire Constabulary was informed of the incident and went to Childwick Hall around 3 a.m. to question the clergyman as to what prompted the unprovoked shooting. Mr Brogden stated that as his house stood in an isolated position, he lived in fear of thieves and he had assumed there had been an intruder. He had met Wintle some months before the shooting and they had agreed that the constable would show a light when on duty in the area so that the clergyman would know who was outside in the dark. But Brogden insisted that on this particular night no light was shown and, although he had shouted twice out of the window for the intruder to reveal himself, he received no reply so fired the shotgun.

At the trial Mr Justice Alderson summed up by saying, 'It was a very foolish and a very rash act, Mr Brogden, and I hope that you will not do such a thing again. I entirely acquit you, in my belief, of any intention of firing to injure any one.' So Revd Brogden was acquitted and PC Wintle made a good recovery.

PC Benjamin Snow of Benington was not quite so fortunate. Nineteenth-century Benington was a peaceful little village whose main peril was poachers, the most notorious of these being a criminal named James Chapman. A warrant for Chapman's arrest had been held at Stevenage since November 1865 and when PC Snow heard that Chapman, a native of Luffenhall some four miles from Benington, was in the area, he was keen to execute the warrant.

Tuesday 10 January 1871 was a bitterly cold winter's day. Snow set out at around midday with two other police constables in search of Chapman, but for some reason neglected to take his truncheon with him, something he would later regret. The policemen split up and Snow began walking towards Sacombe Pound. Chapman, meantime, was cutting across Coombe's Field where he came across James Gilbey, a sixteen-year-old 'intelligent and respectably attired' farm labourer on his way home. Gilbey noticed Chapman was concealing a gun and passed the time of day with him as they walked along. Suddenly Chapman told Gilbey to wait for a moment and disappeared into the field. After a few minutes the sound of a gunshot rang out through the village. Gilbey ran after Chapman and found him making his way back along the lane with fresh blood on his fingers. PC Snow also heard the gun shot and hurried off in pursuit.

Gilbey parted company with Chapman along Bourne Lane and hastened on home. Along the way he passed Snow, but they did not speak. Snow caught up with Chapman and the last thing Gilbey saw was the policeman grabbing Chapman's jacket.

PC Snow was not seen until twenty minutes later when he returned staggering along the lane alone and clutching the left side of his head. He passed villager William Beadle who was in his garden, reportedly telling him, 'Beadle, I am shot,' to which Beadle unhelpfully replied, 'That's a bad job,' and left the constable to go on alone. The injured man was still wearing his hat but blood was running down the side of his face close to his left ear. The policeman finally reached his home in Stoopers Hill at around 1 p.m. and his concerned wife, unable to make any sense of what her husband was saying, at once put him to bed and called for Mr Hodges, the local doctor.

PC Snow had a large zigzag cut on his head and, although Mary Ann Snow persisted in asking her husband what had happened to him, he seemed confused and could only say 'Enemy, got the gun and run away'. After that he was very quiet. As the day wore on the constable lapsed into terrible agony and died shortly after ten that night.

It was found that the skull above his left ear was broken and driven into his brain, which was lacerated from the pressure of a huge blood clot. His hip was injured and his arm was black with bruises as if he had tried to shield himself from heavy blows. Perhaps if Snow had remembered his truncheon that morning he could have defended himself more ably and possibly even survived the attack. The court later heard that it was evident that Snow had received one, if not more, violent blows from some blunt instrument such as the butt end of a gun. The policeman was thirty-two and much respected in the village. He died leaving a wife and three children, the eldest, Mary, being ten years old and the youngest, Lily, only six months.

James Chapman, thirty-seven, was charged with the wilful murder of Benjamin Snow and appeared at Hertford Assizes in March 1871 before Mr Justice Hannen. The defence counsel claimed that as Snow was not in possession of the arrest, warrant when he went after Chapman he had no right to effect a lawful arrest and that Chapman was within his rights to defend himself 'even unto death'. Hannen, in his summing up, came back to this point, saying that if the jury believed Snow's injuries were inflicted in consequence of excitement and provocation produced by his unlawful arrest, they would be justified in finding the prisoner guilty of manslaughter rather than wilful murder. The jury took little time in finding Chapman guilty of

The Bell Inn, Benington where PC Benjamin Snow's body was taken awaiting inquest, 1871. (HALS CV/BEN/10)

manslaughter and he was sentenced to fifteen years' penal servitude. Unwittingly the judge had almost justified the policeman's murder. Chapman remained unmoved during the sentencing.

Mary Ann Snow stayed in the house in Stoopers Hill, marrying George Brooks, another police constable. PC Snow's grave can still be seen in St Peter's churchyard, Benington.

But Snow was not the only policeman to meet an untimely end in the course of duty in Victorian Hertfordshire. 'Horrible Murder of Police Constable John Starkins' declared the headlines in November 1857.

A cold Monday in early November saw several police constables combing Cooper's Braches field near Six Hills, Stevenage, following the last known movements of their colleague who had been missing since before the weekend. As he neared a deep pond in the middle of the field, PC William Isgate noticed what looked like part of a foot sticking out of the water. On going closer, he distinctly saw a hand. With the help of the other constables, the corpse was dragged out and found to be the mutilated remains of their colleague, PC John Starkins. His throat had been slashed so severely that his head was almost severed from the torso and his face had been viciously cut. A reward of £50 was immediately offered for the apprehension of the murderer.

Twenty-five-year-old PC Starkins, a St Albans man, once in the employment of the Earl of Verulam, was stationed at Stevenage police station. He had only been in the police force six weeks when on Friday 30 October 1857 he was instructed to observe the actions of thirty-five-year-old Jeremiah Carpenter, a labouring man working on Norton Green Farm. The farmer, Mr Horn, had suspected Carpenter of robbing him and had requested Starkins follow the man home from work to see if he had any of his master's possessions about him.

Starkins left work at about five that Friday evening, wearing his uniform under a plain overcoat and carrying a pair of handcuffs and a stick. His instructions were to report back at the station at 6 p.m. Witnesses saw Starkins at Wilmore Common, apparently observing a person in the direction of Cooper's Braches field near Six Hills at about 5.30. This was the last time he was seen alive, for when he failed to report to work at the agreed time officers were sent to look for him. The search continued over the weekend without success and it was not until the following Monday morning that his body was discovered in the pond. A patch of grass twenty yards away was heavily bloodstained and trampled down, showing signs of a desperate struggle. Ears of wheat from an adjoining field lay strewn about and trodden into the ground and there were marks indicating something heavy had been dragged along towards the pond. Turnips were discovered, fresh pulled and scattered at the entrance to the field, the inference being that the thief was trying to make off with stolen wheat and vegetables from his master's field when Starkins apprehended him, requesting he show the contents of his basket. The policeman's handcuffs were found open nearby. Police Inspector Hawkes wasted no time in visiting the home of Jeremiah Carpenter.

Police sometimes searched the baskets and wallets of labourers as they left work and Carpenter had often been heard to boast that no policeman should ever search him. He regularly left work at 5.30 p.m. and walked the mile home along the lane from the farm to his cottage. On the day of the murder he left fifteen minutes earlier than usual and was seen making his way through Cooper's Braches field. However, he did not arrive home that night until forty minutes later at 6.10, when by normal calculations based on his ordinary leisurely pace he should have been home by 5.30. When asked to explain this discrepancy later in court, Carpenter said he had walked a longer, more circuitous route, but witnesses later disproved this. He was seen returning home by the back way, limping badly in one leg and with his smock twisted around his shoulders. Nine-year-old William Shepherd, who lived in the next-door-but-one cottage, saw Carpenter come home at about 6 p.m. He said, 'He walked lame as he came up the garden.' Carpenter's wife alerted William's father, who worked with Carpenter, telling him that her husband appeared to have met with an accident.

Mr Shepherd found Carpenter had inexplicably changed from his labouring clothes into his Sunday best and was on hands and knees beside the log pile outside with his right leg between two trunks of timber. Shepherd said, 'I lifted off the wood as quickly as I could and as soon as I lifted it off him, he fell upon his back and said "oh dear, I've smashed my ankle and broke my leg."' This was later thought to be a cover for injuries sustained in the wrestle with the policeman. To explain why he was wearing his Sunday best, Carpenter said, 'I put my best smock on to go and get some victuals but can't go now I've hurt my ankle.' The next day Carpenter went to work as usual but was still wearing his Sunday smock. He was unable to continue and returned home in a greatly agitated state, seemingly preoccupied with the disappearance of the young police constable.

Upon the discovery of the body Carpenter was arrested and his clothes examined. Bloodstains were discovered and a basket splashed with blood was also found in his home, containing a small amount of wheat — the same kind as was found in the field where the struggle appeared to have taken place. Blood was also found under the handle of Carpenter's knife, despite it having the appearance of being washed clean, and its blade matched the size of a cut on the constable's coat collar. Remnants of his working smock-frock with bloodstains were also found in a cupboard in the cottage.

Thirty witnesses were examined on behalf of the prosecution but Mr Serjeant Parry for the defence put up a good case. Parry pointed out that the prisoner regularly suffered nosebleeds and that on the day of the murder Carpenter had been helping to ring some pigs; a good deal of bleeding had occurred during the task, which would have stained his clothes. In the days

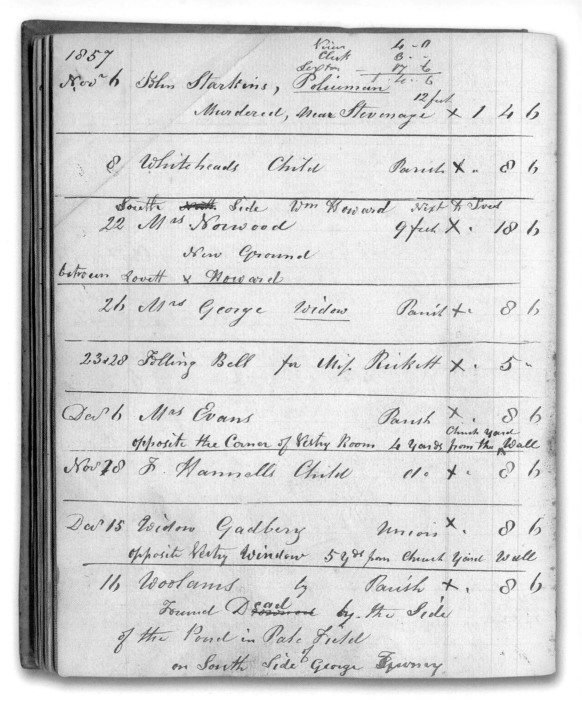

1857

Nov 6   John Starkins, Policeman   Vicar 4 - 0
                                     Clerk 0 - 0
                                     Sexton 17 6
                                            4 - 6
         Murdered, near Stevenage   12 feet   × 1 4 6

         8 Whiteheads Child   Parish × . 8 6

         South   Side   Wm Howard   Next to Trees
         22 Mrs Norwood   9 feet × . 18 6
                New Ground
between Lovett × Howard

         26 Mrs George   Widow   Parish × . 8 6

         23+28 Tolling Bell   for Miss Rickett × . 5 -

Dec 6   Mrs Evans   Parish × . 8 6
         Opposite the Corner of Vestry Room   4 Yards Church Yard Wall
                                                       from the
Nov 18   F. Hannells Child   do × . 8 6

Dec 15   Widow Gadbery   Union × . 8 6
         Opposite Vestry Window   5 yds from Church Yard Wall

         16 Woolams   by   Parish × . 8 6
             Found Dead   by the Side
         of the Pond in Pale Field
              on South Side George Twoney

Burial book of St Michael's church showing the entry for John Starkins. (HALS D/P 92/1/10)

before forensic science, it would have been impossible to distinguish between animal and human blood. Then William Red came forward. He worked with Carpenter sowing wheat. He said of the day in question, 'I was with Carpenter until half past five, quite that or rather more, when he left to go home.' This threw up some doubt as to whether Carpenter could have actually been at the scene of the murder at the time it was believed to have taken place. But then policeman William Quint stepped up to give an extraordinary piece of evidence for the prosecution.

Quint stated that he was accompanying the prison van on its way to jail and overheard Carpenter talking to another prisoner about the Starkins case, saying, 'I done it, but nobody knows it.' However, Quint was about to be cross-examined when he collapsed in a dramatic fainting fit. His collar and coat were immediately loosened but as he did not recover the judge suggested he be removed into a cool room. Some saw the collapse as a sign that Quint had committed perjury and was overcome with guilt. But the *Hertfordshire Mercury* defended the policeman, saying he had not eaten since 8.30 that morning, and the stress caused by the cross-examination and the heat in the court all contributed to his feeling unwell.

Parry then addressed the jury, putting forward that it was indeed a case of 'strong suspicion' but no man's life ought to be taken upon suspicion only. He highlighted the fact that Starkins had been asked only to observe Carpenter on that fateful evening in October as it had been mere supposition that the prisoner was thieving from his employer. He stressed that there was no direct evidence to show that Starkins and Carpenter ever came into contact that night. The jury deliberated for about half an hour and, although conceding that it was a case of great suspicion and despite considerable circumstantial evidence, returned a verdict of not guilty. The Starkins case was regarded as a strong argument for the growing movement against capital punishment.

The *Hertfordshire Mercury*, however, had no doubt of Carpenter's guilt and even before the trial stated categorically, 'The evidence against the man is so conclusive that there cannot be the slightest doubt as to his being the party, or one of the parties, guilty of this atrocious death.' And after the verdict the paper's comment was, 'the woodstealer and the pickpocket are shut up in prison while Cain goes at large, shriven by juries who believe him guilty'.

The funeral of the dead policeman took place at St Michael's church, St Albans, near to where the constable's widowed mother lived. A few months later a gravestone was donated by Hertfordshire constabulary in memory of the man who had faithfully given his life in the line of duty.

9

THE GREEN LANE BABY KILLER

St Albans, 1875

After the execution of Thomas Taylor at Hertford in 1839 Hertfordshire enjoyed a remarkably long period before the gallows were once again employed. There were still a number of offences which carried the death penalty, but, in practice, after 1836 people were only executed for murder or, very occasionally, attempted murder. It was not until 1875 that a murder was committed by George Hill in St Albans that was so terrible that his execution was inevitable.

George Hill was a twenty-year-old groom in the service of farmer Mr Belgrove who had land in Broad Colney in the parish of Shenley. For twelve months he had been seeing Sarah Thrussell, who lived in Queen Adelaide Street, St Albans and was the same age as her sweetheart. On 12 February 1875 Sarah gave birth to an illegitimate son whom she named William George Thrussell. Sarah and George broke up soon afterwards and he began courting a woman named Hannah Kiff from London Colney.

Sarah applied to the St Albans borough magistrates for a bastardy summons to be issued against George Hill to ensure he supported his offspring, financially at least. When Hill learned of this he proposed marriage and Sarah accepted. The magistrates agreed to adjourn the bastardy hearing for a month to make sure the marriage took place. When the case was recalled on 9 June Thrussell asked for a further adjournment because marriage banns were to be published at St Peter's church in St Albans the following Sunday and the wedding date had been set for Monday 5 July, two days before her twenty-first birthday.

The day before the wedding Hill asked to meet Sarah and insisted that she bring the baby. He said he wanted to show her the home he had set up for them. This was not the first time he had made such a request. Previously they were due to meet at Radlett railway station to go to London but Sarah's mother refused to let her take the baby. Shortly afterwards Hill insisted on seeing Sarah and William at the Midland station in Victoria Street, St Albans, adding that she must not tell her mother about it. It was raining heavily on the day of the meeting so Sarah did not take the baby along with her, much to Hill's annoyance. Hill said that if she had brought William along he would have taken them both to their new home. She would have to meet him again the next day and, as he repeated several times, she must bring the baby this time.

They met on the evening of 4 July and walked towards Green Lane which led to New House Farm in the St Peter's parish of St Albans. Hill was pleased to see that Sarah had brought William with her this time and told her she would be back home by nine o'clock if they made haste.

They reached a wheat field and Hill said they could take a short cut through it. When they reached the middle of the field he said he would take her to their new home if she wanted or take her back home. Sarah did not believe that he intended taking her to the new home so replied that she wanted to go home. Hill then complained that his leg ached and thought he should rest awhile on the stile at the top of the field. After resting at the stile Sarah said she was not going to stay any longer. As they reached the bottom of the field Hill said he was not ready to leave yet and placed his arm over the gate to prevent Sarah from leaving.

Hill asked Sarah to go to the side of the hedge with him. When she refused he put his arm round her and marched her there. Upon hearing a cart approaching Hill said they must not be seen there or they would be locked up and suggested they go further into the wheat field until the cart had passed. Hill went into the field first and Sarah followed. When the cart had passed Sarah repeated that she was going to go home. Then she felt a hard blow on the right side of her head.

Sarah partly turned round and said, 'George, what are you doing?' In a reference to the summons he replied, 'I am paying you for sending me that piece of paper.' Hill told her to put the baby down. She refused but he forced her down and she then laid the baby on the ground. Hill knelt beside Sarah, pulled a hammer from his pocket and struck her repeatedly with it. When he thought Sarah was too severely wounded to stop him, he turned upon the baby. Sarah saw Hill strike it once with the hammer but could not bear to watch any more and turned away. Hill placed the dead body of the baby under Sarah's clothes. He asked her, 'Are you nearly gone? Sarah, can you ever forgive me?' She replied, 'Yes; go away and leave me.'

They then heard voices in the lane and Sarah called out 'murder'. Hill raised the hammer to strike her again but she managed to grab hold of it. Hill let go of the hammer and ran off. Sarah managed to struggle over the gate. She saw three young ladies approaching but they fled upon seeing her.

Charles Edwards who lived at New House Farm heard Sarah's cries of 'murder' from the direction of a stile on which he had recently seen a man and a woman sitting. He was not too concerned as he often heard similar cries from children who played in Green Lane, which was a back road between London Colney and St Albans.

Some ten minutes after hearing the cries of 'murder' Edwards heard his dogs barking and a sharp knocking on his front door. He opened it and found

Sarah Thrussell holding a bloodstained hammer which was later identified as a common farm labourer's hammer, weighing 10½ ounces. Her hands and face were streaming with blood, and she told Edwards that her sweetheart had attacked her and her baby and left them for dead.

PC George Woodwards was patrolling that night when he was told of the attack and hurried to New House Farm. Upon entering the yard he saw Charles Edwards coming from the fields holding the body of a baby in a shawl, probably the garment Sarah had discarded during the attack. Woodwards asked Sarah who had caused the wounds to her. She refused to tell him saying only, 'He has killed his baby and has gone,' indicating that George Hill was the murderer.

Woodwards had seen Hill just three hours before the murder when he had walked past the policeman's door accompanied by Hannah Kiff. He went to Hill's house in Broad Colney where he was told by Hill's parents that their son was not at home. Hill had recently been seen by neighbours leaving the house almost naked and going into an oat field.

Just after midnight PC Woodwards returned to Hill's home and this time found him lying in bed between his two brothers. Woodwards said, 'Well, George.' Hill raised himself on his elbows in the middle of the bed and replied, 'Halloa, Mr Woodwards!' Woodwards arrested him for the murder of William Thrussell and Hill responded by saying, 'You told me a few nights ago that I was going the wrong way.' Hill was taken to St Albans police station. There Superintendent Pike was overheard to say, 'Well, Hill, what's all this about?' Hill replied, 'I had a thought come over me that I would kill the girl and the child too, and afterwards kill myself.'

On the supposed day of his marriage George Hill attended a coroner's inquest on the body of his son and a magistrates' court hearing. Hill's expression was grave throughout and once or twice he buried his head in a handkerchief and shed tears as St Albans surgeon Frederick Webster told the court that the baby had died from blows to the head with a blunt instrument. Both courts adjourned for a week.

In between hearings many people visited the scene of the murder. False rumours spread that Hill had made a full confession and had nearly committed suicide by hanging himself in his cell. On 8 July William George Thrussell was buried in the graveyard of St Peter's church.

At the resumed coroner's inquest Sarah Thrussell appeared pale, bandaged, bruised and dressed in black. One newspaper rather unkindly described her as being 'of somewhat common-place appearance'. Frederick Webster had made a post-mortem examination of William Thrussell and found six marks of blows on his scalp. They could have been caused by the hammer. The inquest lasted nearly four hours and resulted in the jury returning a verdict of wilful murder against George Hill.

The following day a resumed magistrates' court hearing took place and a large crowd of mostly women gathered outside the court. Hill again buried

To The Governor   March 24th 1876
County Prison   Church Lane
Hertford   Horncastle
      Lincolnshire

Sir

    Pleas i beg your Pardon in Writing to you
to inform you that i understand that you have
a Prisoner now under the Sentence of Death
at the County Prison at Hertford Sir this is to
inform you that if the Execution take Place. Pleas
i offer to you my Services if Wanted to be the
Executioner of the Prisoner at the Time that is
itnointed if Wanted i Will bring all things that is
Wanted for the Execution Rope and Strapps and
Cap Sir i thought it my Duty to write to you
To Let you now my address and also to Let you
now that on Tusday Next the 28th i shall be at
the County Prison Morpeth Northumberland to
Execute a Prisoner thear and acording to the
Presant araingement i Shall be at the County Prison
Maidstone April the 4th to Execute a Prisoner thair
Sir i have Sent you tow of my Cards Pleas
Will you be so kind as to give Won Card to the
under Sheriff i Shall be glad to reseave a Letter
Either from you or from the under Sheriff
in this Matter as Quick as you Can then
i Shall be able to make all my araingements
Right if Wanted you may Depend on me to be
thair at the apointed Time i Shall Return home
Wendsday next the 29 if all be Well
    Sir i Remain your Humble Serviant
      Wm Marwood
To The Governor   Church Lane
County Prison   Horncastle
Hertford   Lincolnshire

Letter from hangman William Marwood to the governor of Hertford Gaol offering to hang George Hill. (HALS SH2/4/3/39)

63

his head in his hands as the evidence was given. Sarah Thrussell repeated her evidence but found it more difficult in Hill's presence. Hill was charged with the murder of William George Thrussell and the attempted murder of Sarah Thrussell. His trial was to be held at the Hertford Assizes and he was taken to Hertford Gaol on 13 July to await his day in court.

Hill's arrival at Hertford Gaol was a matter of some concern to the governor Frederick George Hankin. He had read the newspaper reports which claimed Hill had attempted suicide and he wrote to the governor of St Albans prison for clarification on Hill's state of mind. While waiting for a reply Hankin employed an extra warder so that Hill could be kept under constant surveillance, and his cell door was not locked so that a warder could get to him immediately should he attempt suicide. Upon learning that the press reports had been false Hankin removed the extra warder, and decided to treat him like any other prisoner awaiting trial.

Hill's trial took place in March 1876 before Lord Chief Justice Coleridge. Besides the murder and attempted murder he was charged with wounding with intent to disable and intent to do grievous bodily harm to Sarah Thrussell. Hill pleaded not guilty to all charges.

Hill's defence readily admitted Hill had committed the murder but tried to suggest that he was insane. His father Saul told the court that some five years ago Hill had sunstroke, and 'He has never been the same man since.' He became 'more excitable and strange in his manner'. Examples of Hill's strange behaviour included running very hard for no reason and running all the way from St Albans by the side of a horse to see which was the faster. He would also sit down for dinner, get up without eating anything and return later to eat part of it. His mother Alice supported her husband's testimony, adding that Hill would cry violently whenever he was scolded. Dr John Evans had seen Hill twice a week during his eight months in Hertford Gaol but had not noticed anything unusual about his behaviour.

The judge summed up the case for 1¼ hours before dismissing the jury who returned after twenty-three minutes of deliberation. They delivered a guilty verdict against George Hill on the charge of murder. The judge said it 'would have been a monstrous thing if you had been acquitted upon the ground of insanity'. The defence's examples of Hill's alleged madness were no stranger than the behaviour of many other people, he said. They did 'not come anywhere near what the law of England required'. Coleridge duly passed a death sentence. Hill, who at times appeared to have been overcome with emotion during the trial, showed no sign of surprise at the verdict.

There was some controversy when the judge passed the sentence for he failed to don the black cap and omitted the words 'May the Lord have mercy on your soul.' Also, by saying to Hill 'I must leave it in hands where it properly may be left, the question whether the sentence I am about to pronounce shall be carried out', some observers were led to believe that he would recommend Hill for mercy and a commutation of his sentence. Rumours also spread that Coleridge had intimated to the High Sheriff that he would recommend Hill for mercy.

As it was thought that Hill would be reprieved it wasn't until the last minute that a petition bearing 200 local signatures was sent to the Home Secretary asking for mercy on Hill's behalf. This was probably owing to the growing national feeling that the death penalty should be abolished rather than any sympathy for Hill's actions. The grounds of the petition were Hill's alleged insanity and the Judge's words, which some interpreted as meaning the sentence would not be carried out. Hill himself had no illusions of being saved and the petition was rejected.

Hill's behaviour in gaol while awaiting death was described as 'most exemplary'. He made a full confession of his crimes which made it abundantly clear that they were premeditated. Hill revealed he had planned the murder some time before he committed it. The initial plan included his suicide but he later decided against this part of it. For some time Hill had been carrying the hammer around with him, waiting for an opportunity to kill his son and former girlfriend. He believed that he had killed Sarah Thrussell as well and therefore he considered himself as guilty of her murder as his son's.

The date of execution was set for Monday 10 April 1876 at 8 a.m. This would be the first execution in Hertfordshire to be held since the 1868 Capital Punishment Amendment Act, which meant it would be held behind prison walls rather than in front of thousands of onlookers, although a number of newspaper representatives had successfully applied for passes to view the hanging.

The governor of Hertford Gaol visited Whitehall the week before the execution to find out if Hill would be reprieved or executed and was told to proceed with arrangements for an execution. Executioner William Marwood arrived at Hertford Gaol on 8 April and took up residence there. Marwood spent most of his time reading but also inspected the drop which had been built under the personal supervision of the county surveyor at a cost of £10 10s.

The night before his execution Hill went to bed just after 10 p.m. and slept soundly until almost 5 a.m. At 7.45 the funeral bell at All Saints church, Hertford tolled. Just before 8 a.m. Marwood pinioned Hill and a procession made its way towards the scaffold. The gaol chaplain led the way reading the burial service. He was followed by the chief warder,

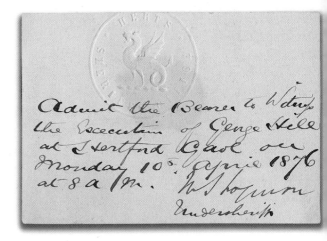

Admission ticket to watch George Hill's execution. This was the first Hertfordshire execution to be held behind prison walls. (HALS SH2/4/3/17)

HERTFORDSHIRE

(TO WIT).

We, the undersigned, hereby declare that Judgment of Death was this day Executed on GEORGE HILL, in the Hertford County Prison, in our Presence.

Dated this Tenth day of April, 1876.

M. S. LONGMORE,
Under-Sheriff.

F. G. HANKIN, Lieut.-Col.,
Gaoler of Herts. County Prison.

H. DEMAIN,
Chaplain of Herts. County Prison.

JOHN ORRIDGE,
Sheriff's Officer.

EDWARD ORAM,
Clerk to Under-Sheriff.

VERNON AUSTIN,
Proprietor of Hertfordshire Mercury.

I, JOHN TASKER EVANS, M.D., the Surgeon of the Hertford County Prison, hereby certify that I this day Examined the body of GEORGE HILL, on whom Judgment of Death was this day Executed in the Hertford County Prison, and that on that Examination I found that the said GEORGE HILL was dead.

Dated this Tenth day of April, 1876.

J. TASKER EVANS, JUN., M.D.

Copy of poster put up outside Hertford Gaol after Hill's execution. (HALS SH2/4/3/12)

two warders, the under sheriff of Hertfordshire, the gaol governor, George Hill flanked by two warders, Marwood and finally more gaol officials.

Hill walked firmly towards the scaffold, his face upturned as if in silent prayer. However, when he reached the scaffold and was placed under the beam he began trembling. Marwood swiftly adjusted the noose and placed the cap over Hill's head before withdrawing the bolt holding the trap door. The black flag was hoisted over the prison for the crowd outside to see. A coroner's inquest was held on Hill's body at 11 a.m. and his remains were buried at 2.30 p.m. the same day.

The death of Hill was not the end of the matter. In May 1876 a question was asked of the Home Secretary in the House of Commons regarding Judge Coleridge's sentencing of Hill. Coleridge had not worn the black cap or said the prayer and some had believed his wording suggested the death sentence would not be carried out. It was also asked how long was it before Hill himself was told there was no chance of a reprieve. The Home Secretary replied that the gaol governor, chaplain and under sheriff had all been instructed to tell Hill the moment they found out, which was one week before the execution.

The Home Secretary did not consider that the judge's words raised false hopes as all responsibilities relating to reprieves were the Secretary of State's alone. While the Home Secretary could not allow an execution to go ahead if the judge had recommended mercy, that was not the case in this instance. Coleridge had told the Home Secretary that Hill had committed 'the most wilful and deliberate murder he had ever tried'. When the newspapers had questioned Coleridge's sentencing in March he had written to the Home Secretary saying that he had never recommended mercy and that the law ought to be carried out.

Before Hill's there had been no hangings in Hertfordshire for thirty-seven years. But the next came just four years later.

10

MURDER AT MARSHALLS WICK

Sandridge, 1880

A hot night in the late summer of 1880, and the inhabitants of Marshalls Wick† Farm at Sandridge near St Albans lay sleeping soundly. At about 3 a.m. on Sunday 22 August sixty-eight-year-old Edward Anstee, farmer, was woken by a noise outside in the yard below. He thought he heard someone calling his name. He got out of bed and went to open the window. Leaning out over the ledge he came face to face with an intruder who was resting a ladder against the wall beneath. Mr Anstee barely had time to call out before he was blasted in the face by a shotgun at close range.

As the shots rang out the servant girl Elizabeth Coleman, who was sleeping in the attic, woke up and went to the window. She could see nothing in the darkness so went back to bed. Presently, though, she was awoken again by strange noises inside the house. The intruder had climbed up the ladder into the murdered farmer's bedroom and was ransacking the room. He then went downstairs in search of valuables. Elizabeth Coleman locked her bedroom door and hid under the sheets.

The housekeeper, Mrs Susan Lindsay, had been sleeping at the front of the house when her bedroom door creaked open and a man entered her room, his face illuminated by the light of an oil lamp which he was carrying. Mrs Lindsay asked where Mr Anstee was and the stranger replied that he had gone to attend to a cow that was sick. He then left the room and went downstairs where Mrs Lindsay heard him crashing around. Suddenly he was back at her bedside again, this time demanding to know where the money was kept. Mrs Lindsay said she did not know and he began pulling at her bed covers, saying he wanted to lie down for a little while. Mrs Lindsay called out for Mr Anstee and the stranger said threateningly, 'I told you, he is out.' She then began calling for the servant girl and the man left. As soon as he had gone Mrs Lindsay bolted her bedroom door and lay listening in the darkness.

† Spelling taken from contemporary newspaper reports. Other sources spell the place as Marshalswick.

The intruder was back downstairs, knocking and banging as if breaking a door open. There had been a spate of daring robberies on farms around the area in the previous two months and it appeared that Marshalls Wick was the latest victim. Mrs Lindsay wondered why the dog, which was tied up in the yard, had not barked. It later transpired that it had been given something to quieten it.

The man was back outside Mrs Lindsay's door again, trying to get in. He seemed angry to find himself locked out. 'Where does Anstee keep his money?' he demanded. Mrs Lindsay had only been staying at the farm a couple of weeks to help out while Mrs Anstee was away visiting friends near Reading and answered truthfully that she had no idea where the money was kept. She told the thief that she did not think there was any in the house as Mr Anstee had been recently paying off debts. This angered the burglar and he began thumping on the bedroom door as if with a hammer, saying, 'You must give me all the money you have got. If you do not, I'll burst the door open and give you a knock on the head.' He also told her he was not alone and there were two or three of them that would 'see to it'. He continued to strike the door, demanding she give him five shillings. Mrs Lindsay did not have that amount about her, but pushed a two-shilling piece between the door and the doorpost. This was not enough for the villain and he asked her for more, but when she insisted she had none he eventually left her alone, and with some relief she heard his heavy footsteps descending the stairs.

Then the house became strangely silent. Mrs Lindsay went and looked out of the window. It was a bright, moonlit night and she clearly saw the man going down the garden with a parcel under each arm. But in ten minutes he was back again, only to disappear with two more parcels.

Mrs Lindsay waited anxiously in her room for almost an hour before feeling it was safe to venture out. She poked her head around the door to Mr Anstee's bedroom and in the moonlight made out a pile of bedclothes under the open window. She saw a foot and part of a leg uncovered and sticking out from underneath the clothes. Elizabeth Coleman, the servant girl, joined her but they left the room without daring to investigate further.

It was now 4.30 and becoming light. Elizabeth Coleman returned to her room to dress and saw George Bailey, the cowman, arriving for work from his home at Hall Heath, a quarter of a mile away. She opened the window and shouted to him to come inside. He was surprised to find the doors open and Mrs Lindsay huddled by an oil lamp at the dining room table. Mrs Lindsay told him what had happened and sent him upstairs to Mr Anstee's bedroom. He pulled the sheet off the dead man's body and saw that his brains had been blown out. The entire left half of his face had been shot to pieces. At first he thought an intruder had got in and had been shot by old Anstee. The only way he could identify the corpse as his master was by a scar on his chin. A later post-mortem examination by the surgeon, Mr Webster, found thirty-seven pieces of shot in the head.

The murder of Edward Anstee at Marshalls Wick Farm, Sandridge, 1880. (Illustrated Police News)

George Bailey searched the house. Several items of silver plate appeared to be missing. He then went outside to the yard. The ladder was still leaning against the wall. Some rungs had been broken off and fresh blood ran down the wall and on to the ground. A hammer, not belonging to the farm, was found nearby.

A lad was sent to St Albans city police station behind the Town Hall and PC Quint of the county police was woken for duty. PC Quint called in Frederick Webster, the surgeon, and the two of them left for the farm at around 5.15 a.m.

Marshalls Wick Farm was a modest-sized building of four bedrooms, drawing room, dining room, kitchen and some rooms in the attic. The Anstees had been resident there since 1860. Built of red brick, the farmhouse stood in an isolated spot, hidden by trees, some of which are still standing today in the car park of a shopping area known as The Quadrant. The house was reached by a long path and amid its rose gardens stood the manor of Marshalls Wick, stretching across the area that is now Marshalls Drive. At that time the now populated area of Marshalswick was just a big house, surrounded by woodland, several farms and some cottages. The name 'Marshalswick' is derived from John and William Marschal, who owned land there between 1271 and 1377, and 'Wick', the Old English for hamlet.

1880 Ordnance Survey map of Marshalls Wick showing the locality of the murder. (HALS XXXIV.VIII)

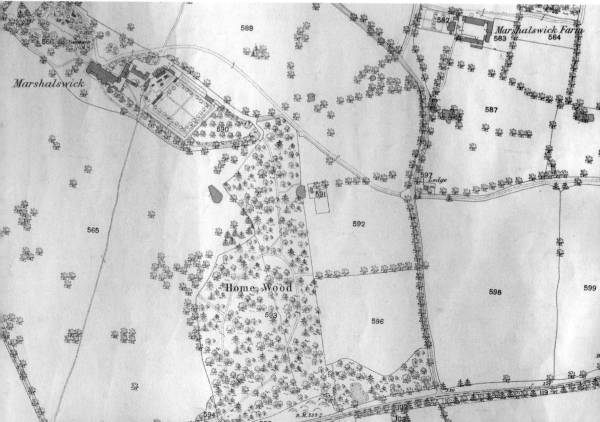

When the horrific extent of the circumstances was revealed to PC Quint and Mr Webster, a message was sent to county police headquarters and more police were drafted in. The man they were looking for was described as being of short stature, around 5 feet 1 inches, aged mid-forties with a reddish complexion, light brown hair turning grey, moustache and wearing a black billycock hat, short brown jacket and brown corduroy trousers. Mrs Lindsay could only describe his voice as being 'extremely peculiar'.

Mr Webster and Superintendent Pike called out photographer Thomas Cooper, at that time living with his wife, eleven children and mother-in-law in Osborn Terrace, New London Road. Mr Cooper was not best pleased to be forced from his bed to work on the Sabbath reluctantly attended but to take photographs. Apparently, though, these failed to do justice to the gruesome scene that had met him that morning, so with the aid of his son he employed photographic trickery on the negative to emphasise the horror.

The police immediately set to work searching the area and within a few hours the stolen silver was discovered in a wheatfield on Evans Farm, less than a mile away. Mr Anstee's Sunday joint of mutton that Elizabeth Coleman had bought from the market the previous day turned up at the foot of Dead Woman's Hill, Sandridge and the gun was found nearby. A trail of investigation, including evidence from several previous robberies on local farms, led police to the man they believed was responsible.

At about 7 o'clock on the evening of Sunday 22 August PC Butterfield of the St Albans City Police went into the Pineapple public house on Catherine Lane (now Catherine Street). There he saw the suspect having a drink with a group of men. He heard the suspect ask of the man next to him whether the things stolen from Mr Anstee's farm that morning had been found. The man replied 'Yes, I think they were found in a shock of wheat in a field called Nine–fields.' PC Butterfield went across the taproom and approached the suspect, asking him if his name was Thomas Wheeler and he replied, 'Yes.' 'Then you are the man I am looking for,' Butterfield said. Wheeler asked, 'What do you want me for?' Butterfield explained that he was taking him into custody on a charge of committing a burglary at a Mr Jacob Reynolds's farm some little time ago. 'I don't know anything about it,' said Wheeler. He was told to finish his beer and accompany the constable.

Wheeler rose and looked hard at the window on the right and the door on the left. Butterfield suspected he was going to make a run for it, so took him by the arm. Wheeler then put his hands on the table and said, 'I'm done. Take me.' Butterfield handcuffed him, then further charged him with another robbery and the murder and robbery of Mr Anstee. Wheeler replied, 'But I have just come out of St Thomas's Hospital' and suddenly began to walk lame. Butterfield told him that if he could not walk then he would carry him. Wheeler said, 'I've done no work; I've got no money,' and then shook his handcuffs as if trying to break them. Word spread fast around the town that a suspect had been apprehended and a crowd had gathered in St Peter's Street as the prisoner was walked back to St Albans police station. Playing to the crowd, Wheeler rattled his handcuffs and 'halloed' to the onlookers.

Thomas Wheeler was born between Wheathampstead and Kimpton and had lived in a cottage at Bernard's Heath, St Albans for some years in the 1860s where he worked for Edmund Smith at Heath Farm. His father died while he was very young but his mother was much respected. Wheeler played truant from school and never learned to read or write. He married in the 1860s at St Albans' Wesleyan chapel and when his home was pulled down in the 1870s he moved to Lewisham. Wheeler was often in trouble; he had been charged with petty theft countless times at Greenwich. Of morose and sullen temperament, he was a drunk and a womaniser, and after abandoning his wife and three children had taken to idly wandering about the countryside, stealing and frequenting the inns. He told Benjamin Welch, an acquaintance in St Albans, that he believed he could get his living without hard work. Wheeler harboured a bitterness about having a great deal of money stolen from him at one time while drunk in St Albans and he vowed to himself to have it all back. A contemporary newspaper reported that his long habits of depravity had blunted all but the animal passions of his nature and he seemed unable to comprehend the enormity of his guilt.

During a five-month spell in Wandsworth prison in January 1880 for stealing butter and eggs, ironically under the false name of Charles Luck, he had plenty of time to plan his spree of farmhouse robberies and was overheard telling another prisoner, 'I was so determined to get what I wanted, I would have killed anyone who stood in my way.'

On 8 June 1880 Jacob Reynolds retired to bed at 8 p.m. Of East Anglian origin, Jacob had taken the lease of Heath Farm in 1870 upon the death of Wheeler's former master, Edmund Smith, and lived there with his wife Ellen and six children until his death in 1926. Jacob was awoken just after midnight by the governess, Miss Marian Yell, knocking on the bedroom door. She said there had been a robbery. Miss Yell had been woken by a noise and thought there was someone in the house. When she looked out of the window she saw the figure of a short man going across the croquet lawn towards the wall. Reynolds went downstairs to the schoolroom. The window looking out to the garden was wide open; drawers were ransacked and lay strewn about and some potatoes had been taken from a sack and lay on the floor in the storeroom. Reynolds returned to bed but the next morning discovered a silver mug with the initials AJR was missing, together with other household items and a Sneider rifle. The value of the articles stolen amounted to around £25. Miss Yell also found a hammer in the flowerbed that did not belong to the farm. This was later identified as one of a pair stolen from blacksmith William Page's shop in St Albans earlier on the evening of 8 June. The other hammer turned up in the passageway of Marshalls Wick Farmhouse on the night of the murder on 22 August.

The stolen items were found by police at the home of Thomas Wheeler's brother Henry soon after the murder of Edward Anstee. Superintendent Pike, following a lead on the recent spate of burglaries, arrived at the Wheeler household, called Raisons near Gustard Wood, on the Sunday morning of 22 August. Henry Wheeler denied any involvement. He said he had been awoken at 3 a.m. one morning in June by someone chucking stones up at the bedroom window. He got up and called 'Hallo! Who's there?' A voice from below said, 'It is Tom,' Henry claimed at first to have no recollection of a Tom, it had been so long since he last saw his brother, but Tom persisted. 'It is Tom. Come down. I have been walking all night. I want some tea.' It was then Wheeler brought in a rifle and a bag and would only say it contained 'something worth money'.

In the early hours of the following morning Wheeler came again with another bag. Henry's wife Anne was uneasy about him storing stolen property at their house and told him as much. Wheeler promised to remove the items the next day and this he did, with the exception of the rifle which remained in the coalhole under the stairs. George Wheeler, Henry's son, had removed it and hidden it beneath some clothes.

Superintendent Pike took Henry and George into custody in St Albans. At his trial Wheeler denied ever having been to his brother's, thus attempting to pinpoint the blame for the Reynolds robbery on Henry.

Thomas Wheeler was also charged with arson at Beech-Hyde Farm, Sandridge on 18 August 1880, where he pilfered a double-barrelled gun and eight pounds of pickled pork but foolishly incriminated himself by leaving a stolen hammer at the scene of the crime. The object was later identified as being the same hammer that had been stolen from John Smith, another blacksmith, of Wheathampstead, around 16 August.

Thomas Wheeler was brought to trial at the Essex Assizes in Chelmsford on Tuesday 2 November 1880 before Mr Justice Hawkins, whose cynical remarks peppered the proceedings. Spectators gathered around the court all day and on arrival Wheeler treated the 'hooting' crowd to a sardonic smile. He was charged with the wilful murder of Edward Anstee. The judge much criticised the trial, stating that the depositions (witness statements made under oath) seemed to have been taken in a 'remarkably slovenly manner' and the fact that no plan of the district had been produced meant he was forced to 'grope his way through the mass of evidence to get some intelligent outline of the case he was presenting to the jury'.

After the murder at Marshalls Wick most of the valuable property was recovered in some wheat stacks standing in a cornfield. The double-barrelled shotgun stolen from Samwell's Farm was discovered by PC Sparks at the edge of woodland at Chandler's Grove, 150 yards away. It had been recently fired. The judge then commented on the 'remarkable coincidence' of the stolen hammers turning up at two scenes of burglary and that it must be surmised that the person who stole the hammers had committed the crimes. The evidence against Wheeler began stacking up.

Mr Webster, the surgeon, said he found a bruise on Wheeler's right arm, which was four or five days old and such a one as would have been caused by the 'kicking' of a gun. PC Worbys of Sandridge found a pair of bloodstained trousers in a meadow adjoining Bernard's Heath on 30 August and gave them to Dr Charles Leymott Tidy, surgeon and forensic lecturer, for examination. Two witnesses confirmed they had seen Wheeler wearing the same trousers on the day before the murder. A waistcoat identified as that belonging to the murdered man was found in Pond Fields some 500 yards from where the gun was found. The bloodstain on the trousers had, in the opinion of Dr Tidy, been recently washed with cold water. He also found bloodstains on Wheeler's scarf. Unfortunately he was unable to ascertain whether it was human or animal blood.

Shots were found in Wheeler's pockets when he was brought into police custody. Much was made of a syringe found on him and which had been identified by several witnesses as belonging to Mr Anstee, who had some hearing difficulties and was recommended to squirt water in his ears. However, Wheeler was most adamant that the syringe belonged to him. By his own confessions Wheeler had often told acquaintances that he hated 'old Anstee' and 'would do for him some day', although he never gave a reason why.

Witnesses came forward to say they had seen Wheeler in the area on the night of the murder. William Little was having a drink in the Painter's Arms public house on St Peter's Street when Wheeler came in. Little offered him a drink and Wheeler told him he had been in hospital having 'wricked' his ankle. This much was true as Wheeler had indeed been admitted to St Thomas's Hospital in London, but was discharged on 8 August, not the 21st as he had led police to believe. They finished their drink and Wheeler said he had 'work to go to' and asked to borrow some money as he hadn't got a penny. Little did not have any money to lend and they parted. Susan Gray of Hatfield Road said she saw Wheeler just after 7 p.m. on the night of the murder and he had asked her for a drink of water. When she refused he swore at her and passed on in the direction of Hatfield. Later, at 9 p.m., Wheeler was seen by William Deamer at Bernard's Heath, carrying a gun.

The next morning at about 11 a.m. Catherine Beatrice Jones was on her way to church with a friend, and as they passed Bernard's Heath they were discussing the murder when a man of Wheeler's description appeared beside them, then passed by and crossed a stile into the fields. He looked at them and smiled in an insolent way which they thought very odd.

Before the police caught up with him at the Pineapple, Wheeler visited a friend, William North, in Adelaide Street. North had not seen Wheeler for at least two years. It was about 3.30 in the afternoon and Wheeler told him he had just come along the road from Luton. Mrs North asked him if he'd heard anything about the murder of Mr Anstee and he replied, 'Yes. I heard of it coming along the road. Poor fellow, it's a shocking job.' Wheeler then asked to borrow a razor and shaved off his beard before inviting North to share a beer with him. He produced a two shilling piece to pay for it. Later, when they heard that the police were looking for him in connection with the murder, North asked him if he'd had anything to do with it, to which Wheeler replied, 'Lor bless you Will, I am as innocent as a baby.'

The judge continued to complain about the depositions saying he had seen 'few taken so badly as those were in this case'. The trial dragged into the following Monday, with the long-suffering jury forced to spend nights on a draughty floor.

In the prisoner's defence it was given that although he was 'undoubtedly a man steeped in crime' much evidence was only circumstantial, and therefore was it enough to deprive a man of his life? The jury clearly thought it was, for after only twenty-four minutes' deliberation they returned a verdict of guilty.

The Judge solemnly donned the black cap, and at the passing of sentence Wheeler fell to his knees in the dock and recited the Lord's Prayer, then requested to speak. 'Please your worship, may I mention one or two words?' To which the Judge replied that it was no use addressing the court now. Wheeler continued speaking as he was taken away, saying something about 'the guilty'.

Wheeler was removed to St Albans Gaol and lodged in the infirmary because there was no cell especially allocated to condemned prisoners, he being the first condemned man to be executed at the gaol. At first he vehemently asserted his innocence, threatening to 'do for' all those who had testified against him. Later he made a full confession and penned a letter to Mrs Anstee, stressing his sorrow for the murder. He was restless and said 'wild' things, threatening to take his own life, but continued to eat and sleep well. His wife and children visited from Lewisham on several occasions, the last being on Saturday 27 November when he was also visited by his brother Henry and his family.

The executioner, William Marwood, arrived in St Albans from Horncastle, Lincolnshire on Saturday 27 November. He had previously executed George Hill at Hertford in 1876. Marwood came to St Albans Gaol on the Sunday afternoon, to observe Wheeler so that he could check his calculations on the correct drop length for Wheeler's weight and height. Wheeler was suspicious as to who the stranger was. He was even more suspicious as to why his cell windows had been whitewashed. But had his view not been blocked he would have spent his last few days staring at his own grave.

Execution was a costly business as fees for the coffin, hangman's rope, pulleys and drivers, tolling bell and Marwood's accommodation all added up to almost £20. However, it was good business for the town as all local tradesmen were employed.

Invoice for Thomas Wheeler's coffin. (HALS SH2/4/1/26)

The night before his execution Wheeler went to bed at 10 p.m. He then got up half an hour later to eat some supper and at 10.50 retired to rest. In the early hours he was restless but then managed several hours of heavy sleep before the chaplain arrived at 6 a.m. on Monday 29 November. Wheeler had some breakfast, although it had been noted that his appetite had fallen off somewhat since Sunday. He later drank his last pint of beer before being taken to the prison yard for execution.

Since this was the first execution that had taken place in St Albans a large crowd of some thousand people had amassed outside the prison walls. The morning was damp and bright and there was full daylight by 7.30. Only bona fide members of the press had been allowed to attend, despite numerous requests being made to the Town Clerk's office. Wheeler's last words were, 'Do remember me to my dear wife and children – my poor dear wife and children – goodbye.' After the execution had taken place a black flag was hoisted above the gaol entrance, and the nearby St Peter's church bell tolled solemnly.

The body of Thomas Wheeler, the man described as a 'cold blooded monster', was placed in a coffin and into the open grave in the prison precincts.

The once peaceful rural area where Marshalls Wick Farm stood is now a thriving postwar housing estate and shopping area, and a petrol station occupies the spot where the farm's duck pond once lay. Only the residential road names now reflect the countryside as it once was, and the nearby Marshalls Wick House was demolished in 1927.

However, this is not quite the end of the story. Wheeler's daughter, Mary Eleanor Wheeler, was fourteen years old when her father was executed and such was her grief that she tried to hang herself from a tree in the garden. Ten years later, under the alias of Mrs Pearcey, she herself was executed at Newgate prison on 23 December 1890 for the murder of love rival Phoebe Hogg in Kentish Town.

11
GUILTY OR INSANE?

One Sunday afternoon in 1882 in the village of Elstree, George Batchelor, a brickfield foreman, was out walking his dogs with a companion, Mr Atkins, when something caught his attention in his brickfield in Barnet Lane. He saw a man peering intently through a hedge on the far side of the field, so went in to investigate. The voyeur slipped away before the two men reached the hedge, but halfway across the field they suddenly came across a stocky young man behind a large stack of bricks, standing over the prostrate body of a young woman who was saturated with blood and moaning in agony. 'Who has caused this?' demanded Batchelor of the man. 'An elderly man was hitting her with a brick', came the reply from the man, George Stratton, who was pulling up his trousers and looked as though he had been involved in a struggle. 'When I came to her assistance, he threw a brick at me and ran away across the meadow.' Batchelor immediately started out to find the villain but Stratton called after him, 'No, no, you won't find him, he has been gone too long.' Instructing Stratton to stay with the injured woman, Batchelor went at once to the police station. When he returned half an hour later with Inspector Thomas Wilson and Sergeant Belderson, Stratton came up to them and said, 'The woman is dead.' A pail of blood-coloured water stood beside the corpse and he had evidently been bathing her face while waiting for the police to arrive.

Around the body lay brickbats and shards of broken bottle covered with blood and hair. The woman's hand was clenched, grasping some of her own hair. Hair was also found torn out and strewn around close by. The body was lying in a pool of blood with the arms extended and the left leg crossed over the right. Fresh blood trickled from wounds on the side of her head and her hair was matted with it. Stratton, a twenty-four-year-old shoemaker from Ivinghoe, Bucks, was immediately taken into custody where Inspector Wilson picked a hair off his boot which was of the same kind as that of the deceased woman.

The identity of the victim was unknown. Aged between twenty and thirty, she was 5 feet tall with dark hair, grey eyes and small hands. Her clothes were old and dirty and she looked as though she had been roaming the countryside for some months. She had first been seen on that Sunday, 13 August, in the Red Lion inn at lunchtime, sitting beside a man named James Freeman. She had offered him half a penny for a share in his dinner, saying, 'That is all I have.' Freeman then gave her part of his food before leaving the inn.

At about two o'clock that same afternoon the woman was seen sitting with two men, one tramp-like, the other stocky, outside the Artichoke pub, laughing and joking and swigging from a bottle. One of the men was John Deakin, thirty-two, a wanderer of no fixed abode; the other, the more muscular of the two, was Stratton. After a while the three began walking up the hill towards Elstree. Stratton had his arm around the woman's waist and they were larking about, the woman knocking his hat off. When they reached the Red Lion on the corner Deakin stopped and hesitated as to whether to continue. Stratton and the woman went on alone for a few yards before he turned to Deakin and said, 'Come along; you're not afraid are you?' Deakin then caught them up as they walked along Barnet Lane. The woman seemed merry and was drinking from a bottle as they passed John Birch, a bricklayer, who recognised Stratton, having worked with him at the brickyard some months previously.

Stratton was then hailed from behind, and on turning saw Inspector Thomas Wilson following them up the lane. He reprimanded Stratton for his use of vile language at Mary Birch's funeral the previous day. Stratton said nothing and the trio continued. Stratton and the woman appeared to be getting on well and she was overheard saying to him, 'You come along with me and I'll take care of you,' at which point Deakin left them and turned back towards the village.

John Birch had now overtaken the group and was sitting on a stile to the brickfield in the sunshine. Stratton came up to him and offered him a drink of beer from the bottle, which Birch accepted. Stratton and the woman then walked into the brickfield and Birch went cautiously towards the hedge so that he would not be seen and watched to see what was happening. They were standing only a short distance away and Birch heard her ask him for money. Stratton replied that he would not give her any and knocked her down. While she was lying on her back with her legs exposed, Stratton began struggling with her and Birch saw that he was 'trying to take liberties with her', which she fiercely resisted. They both rolled down the bank into the hollow and Stratton then kicked the woman violently twice in the head. Just at that moment George Batchelor and Mr Atkins appeared and caught him unawares. The woman was groaning and appeared to be insensible.

Later, when Birch was questioned by police about what he witnessed in the brickfield that afternoon, he was reluctant to give evidence and denied seeing anything. While waiting for Mr Batchelor to return Stratton was observed by Mrs Davies, a police constable's wife, talking to a drunken man who had been asleep in a hedgerow. Stratton said to him, 'I think that little woman is dead and I want you to come and see her.' The drunk replied that he knew nothing about it and only went a few yards with him before saying he would go no further and telling Stratton he should report himself to the inspector at Elstree police station. He described Stratton's appearance as 'wild looking' and in a disordered state. It was later discovered that the drunk was James Freeman, with whom the dead woman had shared dinner not two hours before.

John Deakin was apprehended at about 5.20 p.m. by PC Thomas Dale. He was climbing over a gate near the brickfield and holding his hat in his left hand while wiping his face with his pocket handkerchief. When arrested, Deakin told the constable that he knew nothing about a murder and he had not seen a woman that day. He was taken to the police station and, on passing Stratton in the charge-room, said, 'You can get me out of this.' On examination, Stratton had a large quantity of blood on his shirt and his trousers were torn yet there was no trace of blood on his boots, which would have been expected if he had been kicking the woman in the head. There were no blood marks on Deakin at all.

At about 6.15 that evening Dr William Rogers came to examine the woman's body where it lay on the brickfields. The corpse was taken to the Red Lion to await the results of the inquest. Meanwhile, the police faced the unenviable task of endeavouring to discover the victim's relatives, not easy by any means as she had been terribly disfigured by the attack, her head being almost smashed in. To hinder their job further, the clothes she was wearing had been destroyed, contrary to police orders, by a woman who was left in charge of the corpse.

Stratton and Deakin were held on the charge of wilful murder and appeared at Barnet police court on Monday 21 August. Here, the charges against Deakin were withdrawn as there was no further evidence to offer against him. He stated that after he left Stratton and the woman in Barnet Lane he went into a field and slept, then on waking climbed the gate out of the field and was immediately apprehended by PC Dale. Deakin was cautioned not to leave the court as he would have to give evidence against Stratton.

During the court proceedings Stratton displayed a quick-witted nature, cross-examining the witnesses himself. He induced Mr Batchelor to confess that there had been very little blood on him when Batchelor first came upon him in the field. It was only when he returned with the police that Stratton had more blood on him where he had been bathing the woman's face. Stratton then said, 'That's right, Mr Batchelor, speak up for me.' Batchelor said he had gone for the police and left Stratton alone with the woman because he did not realise her condition was as serious as it turned out to be.

John Birch was reprimanded by the court for not going to the woman's assistance when he witnessed the attack. His answer was that he didn't think it would come to a murder case, and clearly he felt that a man kicking a woman was not sufficient reason to interfere, despite admitting that he saw blood running from several wounds on her head. He stated that he had followed the pair out of curiosity and had denied all knowledge of the affair to police because he was frightened and did not know what to say. He said he was sure that if another person had attacked the woman he would have seen them. It was then his turn to be subjected to Stratton's acute questioning.

Stratton: 'Could you see the woman plainly when I kicked her?'
Birch: 'No.'
Stratton: 'Are you sure I kicked her?'
Birch: 'Yes.'
Stratton: 'Where did I kick her?'
Birch: 'On the head.'
Stratton: 'How do you know?'
Birch: 'I am sure of it.'
Stratton: 'Why?'
Birch: 'By the sound. I could not see the woman because she was lying down, but I am sure it was her head from the sound of it.'
Stratton: 'Is there any peculiar sound when a woman's head is kicked?'
Birch: 'I should think so.'
Stratton: 'What induced you to go away when you thought I kicked the woman on the head?'
Birch: 'I saw Batchelor and Atkins coming.'
Stratton: 'I should think it would induce you to stop rather than to go away. Are you sure you were there at all?'
Birch: 'Yes.'

Birch's answers became more and more hesitant, and finally Stratton accused him of not saying anything to the police until he had heard many people talk about the attack, and then spoke up just to make people think he had been there.

Next to give evidence was Dr William Rogers, a surgeon from Stanmore, Middlesex. At the post-mortem he discovered several terrible wounds on the victim's head and found that the skull had been fractured in two places where the bone was driven into the brain. He concluded that the woman had suffered severe blows that must have been delivered repeatedly because in some places the head was literally smashed. He did not find evidence of any injury on Stratton despite his protestation of being hit with a brick by the assailant before he ran off, although he did discover the prisoner was the subject of a 'frightful and extraordinary malformation'[†] which he believed to be congenital, and could not say what the effect of many years of physical suffering would have had upon his mind. Stratton was committed for trial at the Hertford Assizes in November but still protested his innocence.

The funeral for the dead woman took place in Elstree churchyard on Thursday 17 August at 3 p.m. The unmarked coffin was not taken into the church but was interred in the new burial ground. Some of the village children scattered flowers over the coffin as it was lowered into the ground.

---

† The details have unfortunately not been documented.

The woman's body had not been in the ground two hours when a man named Ebbern,[†] a rat catcher from Church Street, Watford, walked into the police station asking to see the deceased as he believed her to be his daughter Eliza whom he had not seen for eighteen months. She had left home at the age of ten and had refused to work but instead had taken to living 'a loose life'. Many who saw the man thought there was a strong resemblance in his features to those of the murdered woman. Mr Ebbern said that his daughter was twenty-eight years of age and about 4 feet 9 inches with grey eyes. Eventually permission was granted by the Home Office for the body to be exhumed on Friday 1 September at noon. Mr and Mrs Ebbern arrived with their two daughters and the coffin was opened. Mr Ebbern immediately recognised the corpse as that of his daughter. She had a peculiarity about her jaw resulting from a breakage in the bone two years previously. She also had an old injury on her hand and this was hastily examined by Mrs Ebbern and her daughters, but they were too much overcome to look at the face. The lid of the coffin was screwed down and the body of Eliza Ebbern replaced in the earth.

George Stratton had spent periods of time in lunatic asylums and gaols. Orphaned from an early age, he was brought up in the Union Workhouse in Leighton Buzzard, Bedfordshire and spent his youth terrorising fellow inmates and being a complete nuisance to the authorities, getting involved in one lot of trouble after another. Cruelty and cunning were two traits in his character, and he was regularly transferred from prison to asylum only to be discharged after a brief period as perfectly sane. On 20 May 1880 he was brought before a magistrate in a London police court, where he gave a fictitious name, on a charge of attempting to commit suicide. He was discharged only to reappear four months later on a charge of assaulting a policeman, and when he was placed in the cells he succeeded in broke the handcuffs that held him. He then went about demolishing the cell and broke a window when he threw the handcuffs at it. When he was brought before the magistrate the next morning, he seemed more subdued and quietly gave his name before placing his hands on the dock and leaping into the solicitor's well, causing great consternation among the gentlemen seated there. His record also included three more attempts on his life, theft, using vile language and the cruel torture of animals.

In his defence at the Hertford Assizes Mr Wightman Wood addressed the jury, urging that at the most they could only bring a verdict of manslaughter against Stratton in the probability that the woman had been the aggressor, having struggled with him for a few coppers, and that suffering pain from his malformation he struck her the violent blows from which she died. He added

† A rat catcher from Watford named William Ebbern appears in the 1881 census. Listed at the same address is his twenty-six-year-old daughter Eliza.

Elstree Burial Register entry for Eliza Ebborn [sic], giving additional information about her identity discovered after the burial had taken place. (HALS D/P 36/1/17)

that Stratton had been an outcast all his life, knowing no other home but a workhouse and lunatic asylums. Medical supervisors of the various asylums in which Stratton had been a patient were called as witnesses to support the defence that the prisoner was insane. Many spoke of his sudden fits of uncontrollable violence and Dr Samuel Lloyd, medical officer for St Giles Workhouse, said that Stratton was typical of cases where a man may be insane then suddenly get well and be discharged only after a long lucid interval to again become insane. In his experience, very often an insane person was cunning, and if he had murdered a person would be likely to try and blame someone else. However, Dr John Lipscomb, the medical officer at St Albans Gaol where Stratton had been imprisoned, failed to find any symptoms of insanity about him whatsoever during his incarceration.

The jury took forty minutes to return a verdict of guilty of wilful murder and requested that Birch be further reprimanded for not interfering on behalf of the woman. His Lordship then donned the black cap and proceeded to pass the death sentence upon Stratton, who kept interrupting with protestations of innocence and complaints that the trial had been unfair. The judge told him he felt his complaint was unfounded, to which Stratton argued, 'No sir, it is not.' After sentence was passed, Stratton asked, 'Can I speak one word?'

His Lordship: 'No, it is over now.'

Stratton: 'I will speak.'

His Lordship: 'Well, let us hear what you have to say.'

Stratton: 'I can safely say before my God, I am innocent of this.'

He was then taken down displaying the most stoical nonchalance.

Stratton's execution date was set for 20 November 1882. Appeals were sent to the Home Secretary asking that he be reprieved as it would surely be 'shocking to hang a man who was clearly a dangerous lunatic with homicidal tendencies'. Two days before the execution was due to take place, and on the same day as the executioner, William Marwood, arrived in St Albans, a reprieve was sent certifying Stratton insane, and he was transferred to

Telegram notifying the governor of St Albans Prison of George Stratton's last-minute reprieve. (HALS SH2/4/2/55)

Broadmoor asylum for criminal lunatics where he remained until his death on 2 July 1908 from pyelitis, a condition causing inflammation of the renal pelvis.

Long after his reprieve the arguments over his sanity raged on and the villagers of Elstree discussed the murder until every gruesome detail was threadbare. Mr W. Osborn Boyes of the magistrates' clerk's office at Barnet wrote that Stratton's cross-examination of the witnesses displayed 'very little insanity about it, but bore more resemblance to clever reflective'.

More doubt was thrown upon the case when the *Barnet Press* printed a report on Stratton's history, stating that he was a perfect master of the art of assuming lunacy when convenient and remained at asylums during his pleasure, deceiving prison doctors. The newspaper described him as a 'cunning impostor' and revealed that while an inmate of the workhouse he had been known to boast that he could commit even murder with impunity, and so successfully deceive by feigning insanity that he could at any time ensure acquittal and in a short time regain his liberty after being passed through a lunatic asylum.

It will never be known whether Stratton really was insane at the time of the murder or whether this past master of deception had fooled them all once more.

12

THE 'HERTFORD HORROR'

Hertford, 1899

In the early hours of 9 March 1899 a murder took place in Hertford which shook the country, disgraced the police and left the historic county town's reputation in shameful tatters. In a residential street a young woman, twenty-seven-year-old Mercy Nicholls from Ware, was brutally stabbed and left to bleed almost to death in the gutter for several hours while witnesses did nothing, showing an indifference which was described as 'unparalleled inhumanity'. Remarkably, the police also failed Mercy through a series of fatal errors and incomprehensible apathy on the part of the officers, which ultimately led to her death and a momentous reorganisation of the county police force.

It was pouring with rain at 2.20 a.m. on Thursday 9 March. Mrs Jane Papper lay awake in bed in her cottage in Railway Street, unable to sleep, when three screams pierced the silence. She then heard a woman crying out, 'Good God, am I dying? Is there water anywhere?' Mrs Papper lay listening for some time before plucking up the courage to take a lamp to the window. Peering out into the rainy darkness she could see nothing so returned to bed. Presently she heard a man's voice and the sound of heavy boots walking up the yard of the Diamond public house below, but she thought little of it as Railway Street in the nineteenth century was a slum area which saw fights almost nightly.

An hour later at 3.30, a man knocked at the front door of 13 Railway Street, home of musician Frederick Davis and his wife Elizabeth. Mrs Davis leaned out of the window. Below her stood a young man of around eighteen years of age. He called up to her, 'Will you lend me an axe?'

'An axe?' Mrs Davis enquired. 'What do you want with an axe?'

'To chop this woman's head off,' came the youth's reply.

Mrs Davis leaned further out of the window but could see no woman. The lad walked off towards the Young Men's Christian Association and reappeared dragging a woman, Mercy, into the road and lay her in the gutter. Mrs Davis could hear the woman moaning. With a horrified cry of, 'Oh you brute!' Mrs Davis screamed for the police as loudly as she could. The man raved, 'The Prince of Wales has got no money; Queen Victoria has got all the money.'

At that moment Henry Wright, the milkman, and his son passed by in a pony and trap with a lantern. Mrs Davis shouted to him to fetch the police. The young man was dragging Mercy up and down Railway Street, picking her limp body up and letting it fall to the ground before proceeding to kick at it. Henry Wright turned his light on to the man and noticed something shining in his right hand. His seventeen-year-old son Ebenezer recognised him at once as 'Rotten' John Smith, a labourer from Aston who was training to be a militiaman. Henry Wright rushed off to the police station, about a quarter of a mile away, instructing Ebenezer to keep watch on the man to see where he went. Smith was still shouting about the Prince of Wales, stating that if he had been there that night he would have stabbed him too.

In a courageous move Ebenezer approached Mercy, and saw that she was completely naked except for a piece of her dress which had been laid across her chest. She was bleeding profusely from the face. He waited about half an hour alone in the street, save for Mrs Davis and a couple of other curious onlookers peering out of their windows. When he was asked later if he'd been frightened, Ebenezer replied, 'No. I would have gone for him if I had had a stick.'

Henry Wright arrived at the police station at 3.40 and spoke to the officer on duty, PC Robert Sherwood. He told him, 'There's a man killing a woman, if she's not already dead, against Mrs Davis's near Bull Plain.' Sherwood's reply was that he could not leave the station until PC Langstone returned but he expected him at any moment. Satisfied that the police would be on the scene any minute, Henry Wright returned to his cart and he and his son drove through Railway Street on the way to milking the cows at Ware. By this time Mercy had been dragged into Diamond Yard and Smith was picking her wet clothes up off the road.

But the police did not arrive and witnesses continued to gawp out of their windows, but did nothing to help Mercy Nicholls. Francis Charles Burton of 9 Railway Street, boot maker and town councillor, was also woken at about 3.30 that morning by the sound of a woman crying 'help me'. He got up and opened the window and saw Smith kicking Mercy and shouting, 'If I had my gun I would shoot her.' Burton was relieved to hear a man below say that the police were on their way, and after watching Smith drag Mercy up and down the street for some quarter of an hour he returned to bed. He later said he had thought it was two tramps fighting. Meanwhile Smith was marching along like a sentry shouting 'Left, left, left. Let 'em come and I will give it to 'em.'

Next on the scene at around 4 a.m. was town lamplighter Charles Papper, whose wife Jane had already heard Mercy scream almost two hours previously. Smith was doing a mock drill in the middle of the road and challenged Papper to 'Halt! Who comes there?' to which Papper replied 'Morning, Sir' and continued on his rounds towards Bull Plain. Smith followed for about thirty yards before turning back to continue marching up and down. In half an hour Papper came back and heard a woman cry out 'Help!' several times. He saw her near-naked form lying in the gateway against Mr Elliott's shop and noticed that she had been stabbed about the face many times. Her clothes lay about six feet away. But Papper was afflicted with the same apathy as the other onlookers and seemed to believe that putting out his lamps was more important than helping Mercy. He later explained that he was frightened and confused and didn't know what to do and didn't think he was allowed to touch the injured woman until the police had arrived.

About 4.40 Job Edwards, also a lamplighter on his rounds that morning, ran into Papper, who told him about the attack. Edwards asked him if he had helped her and Papper replied that he had not because there were gypsies in Diamond Yard. Edwards told him to go to the police but still Papper was reluctant, fearing that he too may get stabbed if he did so, and continued on his rounds. Edwards went to the police himself, arriving at 5.15 and told PC Sherwood that there was a woman in the street with her clothes torn off her. Sherwood's reply again was that he could not leave because he was on duty, but he expected PC Langstone in directly, adding 'he ought to be here now'. Edwards returned to Diamond Yard and saw Mercy lying on her right side. He struck a match and she said, 'Oh Jack, Jack.' Charles Bailey, on his way to work at the corporation yard at about 5 a.m., had been trying to cover her with her torn, wet clothes and resolved to go to the police himself. In the meantime Edwards tried to get some sacks to cover Mercy, but despite asking Mr Elliot, the baker, no sacks were forthcoming.

The notorious Railway Street, Hertford, in 1899, where Mercy Nicholls lost her life. (Reproduced with permission of Hertford Museum)

PC Sherwood was still on duty when Bailey strode into the police station. He told the policeman that there was a woman very much cut about. Sherwood reportedly seemed quite surprised, jumped up and blew his whistle and spoke up the speaking tube, alerting sleeping officers in an upstairs room, saying there was a row up Railway Street and they would need an ambulance. So it was finally at 6 a.m., two and a half hours after the attack had first been reported, that PCs Sherwood and Hewitt arrived at the scene.

By now quite a crowd of people had gathered around the Diamond Yard archway. Charles Papper had returned to Mercy and was waiting with her as the policemen arrived. Smith, however, had disappeared. PC Hewitt bent over the groaning Mercy, who was almost unrecognisable, her hands and face covered with blood. She was put on a stretcher and taken to Hertford Infirmary. A man named James Saunders found a pocket knife lying in a pool of congealed blood and handed it to PC Hewitt. This was later identified as belonging to Smith.

James Saunders then returned to his lodgings at the Coachmaker's Arms in Cowbridge, where Smith was staying, and announced, 'Some poor woman has "copped it" in Railway Street' to Smith and fellow lodger Thomas Montagu, who were sitting down in the kitchen. At this point Smith jumped up, saying, 'Yes, I done it.' Saunders noticed his clothes and boots were splashed with blood and that he was muttering something about losing his knife. Together with Montagu and another lodger, George Brown, Saunders took Smith to Diamond Yard for him to verify the scene of the murder. Smith proudly announced, 'That's where the Prince of Wales died.' The three lodgers then marched Smith to the police station and handed him over to PC George Hart. When Smith was cautioned he replied, 'Yes I stabbed her in case they put me on guard in the Militia,' at which point PC Hart locked him up.

Mercy Nicholls died at Hertford Infirmary at 9.30 that morning. She had been stabbed fifty-nine times in the face, had a deep wound in the throat and was covered in bruises on the knees, spine, left temple and chin. Ten wounds had been inflicted on her left hand and one on the right which was sliced clean through. There were two severe stabs in the chest between the ribs. Dr Roach of Hertford infirmary believed her death was caused by haemorrhage and exposure to the cold and rain. He concluded that had she been attended to just two hours earlier, she would have undoubtedly recovered.

Mercy had been married to brickmaker Samuel Nicholls for six years but for the past two to three years they had separated on many occasions because Nicholls physically abused his wife and Mercy often went to stay with her mother in Cole Green, which is where she had been on this occasion. Her mother, Sarah Ann Carter, stated that she last saw her daughter on the afternoon of Tuesday 7 March when she had said she was leaving to return to her husband, yet she obviously decided to remain in Hertford for the following day, for reasons unknown.

With the murderer freely confessing his guilt and safely behind bars in St Albans Gaol, the press and public turned their attentions to the actions of the people of Hertford and the police and why no one had come to the scene until four hours after the attack had begun. In a disgusted outburst, the *Hertfordshire Advertiser* questioned 'what species of barbarian inhabited this county town where neighbouring house-holders can hear screams and groans in the street but as it was only a woman being done to death, they return to their comfortable beds'.

Railway Street was a notorious trouble spot. Lined with rotten little cottages, some with the windows broken, alleys, courts and yards, it was well known for harbouring disease. A report on the sanitary conditions in Hertford in 1850 contained accounts of decaying buildings, crowded tenements and open sewers, and

Lieutenant Colonel Henry Daniell, Chief Constable of Hertfordshire Police, responsible for creating one of the most efficient forces in the country following the murder of Mercy Nicholls. (HALS, Herts Leaders Social and Political.)

only four years before the murder the area was branded 'Hideous Hertford' with a 'foul labyrinth of pestilential filth, squalor and misery, where no prudent person ventures alone, even by daylight'. Fights were a regular occurrence and some people leaving the taverns and drifting back towards the Workhouse would spend the night lying in the road. But in 1899 only one policeman patrolled this beat, known as beat number one, throughout the night from 9 p.m. to 6 a.m. This officer was PC Herbert Langstone. On the night Mercy Nicholls was murdered Langstone claimed to have walked along Railway Street several times, passing through the last time at 1.30 a.m. He continued his patrol and then returned to the police station at 3.30 where he told PC Sherwood that he was wet and would keep on the move, patrolling a different area of the town.

Where he went after this is a mystery for he was not seen again on his beat and failed to book off duty at 6 a.m. It was the first time this had happened and the Chief Constable, Lieutenant Colonel Henry Daniell, thought this a 'curious coincidence'. Langstone swore on oath at the inquest that he followed his beat until 6 a.m. but went home without signing off because he was soaked through and it had been so quiet. How then had he come to miss John Smith who had spent the greater part of the night stabbing Mercy Nicholls to death in Railway Street in an attack which lasted several hours?

The coroner, Thomas Joseph Sworder, frankly told Langstone that he was sorry but he did not believe his story, and that he thought it probable that he went quietly home to bed and slept the remainder of the night, or he had been 'lying up somewhere he ought not to have been'. But Langstone continued to assert he was telling the truth.

More discrepancies showed up when PC Sherwood was questioned. He maintained that milkman Henry Wright had been wrong about the time he had come to the police station to first report the attack and that it had been 4.30 and not 3.40 as he had stated. When Mr Wright was recalled he said that by 4.30 he had already milked four cows down at Ware and he was certain of the time. PC Sherwood also said that Job Edwards came to the police station much later than he had stated and that two of the witnesses had never come at all. Only a week before the constables had received strict instructions from Superintendent Parish that in cases of burglary, fire or murder the duty constable was to call the Superintendent or Sergeant Gardner, both of whom were sleeping in the police station in rooms connected to the front office by means of the speaking tube. When asked why he did not call for help when Wright first reported the incident, Sherwood said that he had not believed it to be that serious. Both PCs Sherwood and Langstone were dismissed from the constabulary.

After a gruelling ten and a half hour inquest the jury found Smith guilty of murder and added an additional recommendation that they believed the conduct of both constables 'deserving of the greatest censure and their evidence is not to be relied upon. We exonerate the rest of the police from any blame.' A full enquiry by the Standing Joint Committee (Hertfordshire's Police Authority) was subsequently carried out and it was found that constables alone were responsible for patrolling their beats, with no one checking whether they were carrying out their duties properly. It was recommended that there should be more police officers to patrol trouble spots such as Railway Street and more efficient keeping of the attendance books at police stations. The Chief Constable of Hertfordshire, Lieutenant Colonel Henry Daniell, acted swiftly and implemented the recommendations almost overnight, completely re-organising the Hertfordshire constabulary. When he retired in 1911 he was credited with shaping 'one of the most efficient forces in the whole kingdom'.

Slowly the events of the night that became known throughout the country as the 'Hertford Horror' began to slot together. It appears that Smith had been thrown out of his lodging house about 9.30 p.m. for quarrelling with a fellow guest. Then at about 10.45 that night he knocked on the door of Graves's lodging-house and spoke to his aunt, Susan Maynard, looking for accommodation. Mercy Nicholls was with him and spoke to Maynard, appearing the worse for drink, but Smith was apparently sober. The lodging house was full so they both left. They were seen beneath the archway in Railway Street between 11 p.m. and 12.15 p.m. and appeared to be having a friendly conversation. What happened between 12.15 and 2 a.m. that provoked Smith's vicious and seemingly motiveless attack is unknown.

For some time previously Smith had been the gardener to the vicar of Little Berkhamsted and attended church regularly. He mixed freely with the villagers and excelled at cricket. He then found employment on a farm near Hatfield and afterward came to Hertford doing machining work and living in various lodging houses. It was here he fell in with a rough crowd and it is said his character changed. Smith appeared in court in June 1899 and was described as a simple-looking youth of the agricultural labourer type. He wore dark clothes with a red handkerchief around his neck and his face was bronzed. He seemed to take very little notice of the position in which he was placed, was very quiet and did not at all resemble a murderer. He was of small stature and it seemed incredible to the jury that this slight man could have caused such fear in all those men who saw him attacking Mercy Nicholls. He was examined by Dr Boycott, the medical superintendent of the Hertfordshire Asylum at Hill End, and considered to be of unsound mind. Indeed, it was doubtful if he was in a condition to plead at all or whether he really understood the nature and the seriousness of the charge made against him. Dr Boycott came to the conclusion that Smith was 'weak minded' and suffered from delusions. Smith had a family history of insanity with two relations dying in asylums and a background of a series of marriages between cousins. The jury found Smith insane and unfit to plead and he was ordered to be detained during Her Majesty's pleasure. Smith was sent to the Hertfordshire Asylum but was later transferred to Broadmoor. Only after Smith's arrest was it discovered that he and Mercy Nicholls had in fact been related as distant cousins.

The funeral of Mercy Nicholls took place at St Andrew's Cemetery on the afternoon of Sunday 12 March. The body had been removed to the cemetery chapel the evening before and the coffin lid was removed so that Mercy's husband, mother, two sisters and brother could bid a final farewell to her. A large crowd attended the funeral itself and some men from Ware, Mercy's home town, gave vent to their feelings by driving a cart through Railway Street displaying a black flag.

13

MURDER AT THE ASYLUM

Abbots Langley, 1899

In October 1870 a new lunatic asylum opened in Hertfordshire. Leavesden Asylum was just north of Watford in Abbots Langley. It was large enough to house 2,000 patients but none of them were from Hertfordshire. The asylum was run by the Metropolitan Asylum Board and was for London imbeciles. In 1899 one of the patients was murdered by eating a poisoned cake that had been sent to her by post. The final outcome of the case created nationwide controversy. Thanks to the recent release of Home Office papers the full story can now be told.

Caroline Ansell was admitted to Leavesden Asylum in October 1894. In 1899 she was twenty-six years old and still an inmate in the asylum. The beginning of the year saw two disturbing occurrences. On 22 February Caroline received a parcel in the post containing tea and sugar. When she made a cup of tea with it the taste was so bitter that she threw the rest down a sink. Then two days later a letter addressed to Caroline arrived that read:

MARY ANSELL.   THE DEAD SISTER.   MR. ANSELL.

Mary Ansell and her family from the Illustrated Mail's *campaign to prove she was insane and prevent her execution. (*Illustrated Mail*)*

'Dear Carrie

I now send these few lines to tell you that your father and mother is dead. They died last week, and I am very sorry for you and they dear little ones that are left.

I remain, your cousin,

Harriet Parish.'

Neither of Caroline's parents was dead. Harriet Parish was her cousin but knew nothing of the letter and it was not written in her hand.

On 9 March Caroline received another postal parcel. This one contained an unremarkable-looking cake some half an inch thick with a very yellow substance in the middle. There was no accompanying note to indicate the identity of the sender. Caroline did not eat it until the next day when she shared it with three fellow inmates. Two of them ate their pieces but soon vomited. The other inmate spat her piece out. Caroline ate all of her portion, which amounted to half the cake. She soon fell seriously ill, suffering from abdominal pains and headaches, as did inmate Mary Smithers who later ate the rest of the cake. Caroline also began vomiting and her eyes turned yellow. She was admitted to the asylum infirmary four days later by which time her lips had turned black. She showed symptoms of biliousness and peritonitis and by 8 o'clock that night she was dead.

On 16 March Caroline's mother Sarah and younger sister Mary Ann, a servant from London, went to the asylum where they were asked if they would consent to a post-mortem to establish the cause of Caroline's death. The doctor explained that he believed the cake she had eaten was the cause. Sarah said she would have to consult her husband James and get back to him. The next day the doctor received a letter:

SECOND SISTER.

THIRD SISTER.

MRS. ANSELL.

'Dear Sir.

For why do you want a post mortel [sic] examination on the body after being under your care four years? We decline to give you the authority to hold one.

I remain yours,

MRS ANSELL'

It later emerged that Sarah Ansell was illiterate. The Watford coroner Thomas John Broad thought that there was enough suspicion surrounding Caroline's death to warrant a post-mortem and ordered one to take place.

Superintendent William Wood of the Watford police took charge of the investigation into Caroline Ansell's death but had little to go on. He ordered two constables to search the asylum for the discarded brown paper cake wrapper and after a couple of days it was found in a rubbish heap in the asylum grounds. It bore two penny stamps and a WC (London) postmark which was the district where Mary Ann Ansell lived.

On 6 April Wood arrested Mary Ansell for the murder of her sister. She told him, 'I know nothing whatever about it. I am as innocent a girl as ever was born. I have not written to my sister for months; we were never friends. I never sent her anything but a birthday card.' Ansell had a piece of blue paper in her pocket which she said was a list of questions she was going to ask at the inquest. The list questioned Leavesden Asylum's handling and treatment of Caroline's illness and death.

At a coroner's inquest held at the asylum to establish the cause of Caroline's death overwhelming evidence of Mary Ansell's guilt emerged. Home Office pathologist Dr Thomas Stevenson had established Caroline's death was the result of phosphorus poisoning. A shop assistant told how Mary had bought a penny bottle of phosphorus in March, ostensibly for killing rats. She had previously bought four or five similar bottles but her employer, Margaret Maloney, had not instructed her to do so. The Maloneys' house was seldom troubled by rats, and when it was traps were used.

Then insurance agent John Cooper revealed that in September 1898 Ansell had insured her sister's life so that she might give her a decent funeral when the time came. Mary had told him that Caroline was a general servant at Leavesden and decided on a policy that would pay out £11 5s if Caroline died a natural death after 6 March 1899. When Cooper read of Caroline's death in the newspapers he realised Mary had given him bogus information and told her he would repay her premiums if she would return her policy and premium books, but she had burnt them by accident.

Finally, a handwriting expert declared that the letter allegedly from Harriet Parish, the letter refusing a post-mortem and the writing on the cake wrapper were written by the same hand, although the writing on the wrapper was disguised. The coroner's jury believed Mary Ansell was responsible for her sister's death and returned a verdict of wilful murder against her. At a subsequent magistrates' court hearing the evidence was presented again and Ansell was committed for trial at the next Assizes.

Mary Ansell was tried for murder at the Hertford Assizes in June 1899. When the charge against her was read Ansell replied, 'Not guilty, my Lord,' in a firm and determined voice. She denied any knowledge of the Harriet Parish letter, the cake or the tea and sugar. Ansell claimed to have told her mistress of a rat problem but had been ignored. She did admit to having written the letter to the asylum refusing permission for a post-mortem. Ansell explained that she was engaged to be married at the time of Caroline's death but her fiancé was not earning enough for them to set up home together. From this information the prosecution proposed a financial motive for Caroline's murder. They said it was done to gain the insurance money.

The jury returned a guilty verdict against Mary Ansell. The judge donned the black cap and said, 'It is impossible that the jury should return any other verdict than the

The execution of Mary Ansell at St Albans Prison. (HALS Off Acc 688)

verdict of guilty. It had been shown to their satisfaction that you deliberately took the life of your sister. . . . Never in my experience has so terrible a crime been committed for a motive so utterly inadequate.' Ansell was sentenced to hang on 18 July. This was later changed to the 19th when it was discovered that hangman James Billington was at Winchester on the 18th to execute Charles Maidment who had shot his ex-fiancée, and he couldn't get to St Albans prison in time to execute Ansell.

As the news of Ansell's sentence spread so the stories of her diminished mental state began to circulate. The *Daily Mail* mounted a vigorous campaign to prevent the execution from taking place. They began by declaring, 'There can be very little doubt indeed that the condemned girl Mary Ann Ansell is not responsible for her actions.' A neighbour of Ansell informed the *Mail*, 'I assure you that insanity runs in the family. You needn't be a medical man to find that out.' St Albans prison chaplain the Reverend Henry Fowler made daily visits to Ansell who was there awaiting execution. He told the *Mail*, 'I really cannot say that she understands the gravity of her offence.'

Acting on this information the *Mail* compiled a truncated family tree of the Ansells showing how madness ran in the family to illustrate the 'remoteness of her chances of inheriting normal intellectual faculties'. There was Mary's grandmother who was rendered weakminded from being shut in a dark room when a child. Her mother had two aunts who died in an asylum. Caroline had been an inmate of an asylum and an application had been made for her other sister named Martha to be taken into Leavesden.

Mary's employers for the last five years, the Maloneys, wrote to the *Mail* endorsing their campaign. Margaret Maloney had no doubt 'as to Mary Ann Ansell's weak and irresponsible state of mind'. Her husband Patrick wrote that 'I have always had an impression that she was more or less mentally deranged.' Others who knew Mary also gave examples of her state of mind. Mrs G.W.A. Eayres had taught Ansell at Manchester Street Board School between 1886 and 1887. She recalled, 'I always looked upon her as one of feeble, if not irresponsible mind.' Ansell was not allowed to sit behind other pupils as she would stick pins into them. She possessed 'a most insane look . . . and would stare out from under her half-closed lids in the strangest way'. The school's headmistress later distanced herself from Eayres's comments by saying Ansell had passed all of her exams and always appeared sane to her. However, both of them earnestly hoped she would be reprieved.

As the day of the execution drew nearer the *Mail* stepped up its campaign and repeated its arguments again and again: 'Mary Ansell is insane; of that there is no doubt.' Along with their sister publication the Sunday *Illustrated Mail* they listed recent cases in which women had been sentenced to death and reprieved.

On 14 July the newspaper printed an unflattering picture of Mary Ansell under which they wrote, 'Is that the face of a sane person? Is not madness pictured in every line of it? Ask any specialist in brain diseases what he thinks of a face and head of such conformation and in all likelihood he will tell you that the chances are 100 to 1 that the owner is an idiot.' The well-known psychiatrist Dr Lyttleton Stewart Forbes Winslow was shown the picture. From it he concluded that Mary Ansell was a 'typical specimen of a mental degenerate of the lowest order. . . . Her whole type appears to be between a criminal and a lunatic.'

Forbes Winslow had formerly been an asylum keeper and had been educated partly at Berkhamsted Grammar School. He took a keen interest in the Ansell case and it was not the first time he had declared a murderer awaiting execution to be insane. He was surprised that Ansell's defence had not pleaded insanity on her behalf at the Assizes. Her lawyer Percy Wisbey explained that if he had convinced a jury Mary was insane then she would have been sent straight to Broadmoor criminal lunatic asylum for life. If he had used insanity for a defence and failed to convince the jury then there was no alternative defence for him to use, and she would have been found guilty and executed.

Wisbey consulted Forbes Winslow who said that from what he had read he was of the opinion that Ansell was mad and therefore must not hang. Wisbey asked the Home Office for permission for Forbes Winslow to see Ansell inside St Albans prison, but this was refused as only experts nominated by the Treasury or connected with the prison were entitled to do that. Undeterred, Forbes Winslow gathered what information he could and drew up a four-point report:

1. Hereditary insanity. Of this there is not the slightest doubt. She is a mental degenerate so often seen in families where insanity exists, as in hers, to any great extent. Such an individual is allowed her freedom, being simply regarded by her family and neighbours as a weak-minded poor fool, but harmless, and there being nothing objective in her condition she is not, like her sister, incarcerated in a lunatic asylum. There are two insane sisters, and insanity inherited both on the father's and mother's side.

2. Motive. There is generally method in madness, and often motive in an act of insanity. I think that too much has been laid on the insurance policy for £11. At the time she was contemplating the deed very possibly some insane idea was passing through her so-called mind.

3. Behaviour during trial. This was in my opinion most important. There was an absence of excitement or emotion during the whole proceedings, and an inability to realise her condition or the gravity of the act. The summing up of the Judge and sentence of death did not in any way affect her. This is most unusual, even in hardened criminals.

4. Indications of insanity. Intense passion and love alternating with each other. Frequent attacks of mental vacancy. Talking to herself in an incoherent manner, strange hallucinations, loud fits of laughter for no reason.

Winslow concluded 'that Mary Ann Ansell was a mental degenerate, and ought not to be held responsible in the eye of the law'.

Two petitions were sent to Home Secretary Sir Matthew White Ridley appealing for mercy. The first was circulated in Hemel Hempstead and attracted 150 signatures headed by the vicar of Hemel Hempstead. The second was compiled by the *Daily Mail* and was signed by 500 people. The Home Secretary, much to Forbes Winslow's surprise, rejected both. The psychiatrist was now saying that Ansell was 'absolutely insane'. Both the doctors who had examined Ansell were from Broadmoor asylum and a story emerged that Broadmoor was so full that they were not keen to take in any more patients.

The *Daily Mail* received over 10,000 letters in support of their campaign, including one from Charles Cusworth of Capel Road, New Bushey, who had been the foreman of the jury at Ansell's trial. Cusworth wrote, 'If her counsel had urged the plea of insanity, and had put before us the evidence which has since been published, we should have been unanimous, I am sure, to recommending a commutation of the death sentence to a punishment other than a capital one. We had no idea she would really be hanged.' Another juror, Henry Wise from Elstree, wrote independently that 'I fully expected that Ansell would be reprieved. So confidently I expected her sentence would be modified that I thought no word of mine could make the slightest difference.'

The day before the execution two final desperate attempts were made to prevent it taking place. A spontaneous petition was drawn up in the House of Commons and signed by 100 Members of Parliament. All it asked for was a postponement of at least one week so that further inquiries could be made into Mary Ansell's mental condition. The Home Secretary rejected it.

Finally a public meeting was held at the Cannon Street Hotel. A crowd of hundreds gathered but for unknown reasons the hotel had cancelled the booking of the large hall leading many to believe the meeting had been abandoned. A member of the remaining crowd (which included jury foreman Charles Cusworth and Forbes Winslow) cried out, 'They must not hang an innocent servant girl.' It galvanised the by-now-outdoors meeting and former Chief Justice of the Bahamas, Mr Yelverton, was chosen to be the chairman.

A delegation of seven was formed and they quickly made a plan of action. Their first goal was to see the Home Secretary immediately. If that failed they would go the House of Commons and demand to be heard. As a final resort they would go to Windsor Castle to ask Queen Victoria for mercy on Mary Ansell's behalf. Their plan was a complete failure. The Home Secretary was not at the Home Office, nor at the House of Commons. The delegation spoke to the Under Secretary of State for the Home Department who told them that the Home Secretary had already carefully considered Ansell's case. They did not go to Windsor Castle and Queen Victoria had already rejected an earlier appeal, explaining that her Home Secretary was the only person who could deal with such things.

There had been enormous pressure on the Home Secretary from the public, press and his fellow parliamentarians to commute Ansell's death sentence.

CERTIFICATE OF SURGEON.

31 *Vict. Cap.* 24.

Hertfordshire to Wit

I *Eustace Henry Lipscomb* *M.B. B.C. (Cantab), M.R.C.S. Eng. L.R.C.P. Lond* the Surgeon of Her Majesty's Prison ~~of~~ *at Saint Albans in the said County of Hertford* hereby certify that I this Day examined the Body of *Mary Ann Ansell*, on whom Judgment of Death was this Day executed in the said Prison; and that on that Examination I found that the said *Mary Ann Ansell* was dead.

Dated this 19th · Day of *July* 1899

(Signature) *Eustace H. Lipscomb*

Certification that Ansell's execution had been carried out successfully. (HALS SH2/4/2/11)

They appeared to have put forward a reasonable argument about Ansell's sanity, so why did Matthew White Ridley resolutely refuse to consider their appeals? The answer can be found in a Home Office file that was only opened to the public in the year 2000.

The file contains a report written by Broadmoor doctors Nicolson and Berry who had interviewed Mary Ansell. They revealed that Ansell had confessed to sending Caroline the poisoned cake and also the tea and sugar which was laced with oxalic acid. She thought that Caroline's death would not be investigated as she was 'out of the way' in an asylum. The murder was premeditated, 'with the express object of obtaining the insurance money having in her mind at the time the intention of possibly taking her sister's life in order to facilitate arrangements for her own marriage'.

Vitally, the doctors thought Ansell was sane, 'and is in no sense the imbecile that she has sometimes been reported to be. She answered all questions intelligently.' Two lines were underlined in blue pencil, possibly by Ridley himself. Firstly, where the report said Ansell 'had never been insane, and we were unable to detect in her existence of any delusion, hallucination, or other indication of mental disease'. Secondly, where it was reported that the matron at St Albans prison had said that in the three months she had known Ansell she 'had not exhibited any symptoms of insanity'. This opinion was shared by the chairman of the prison visiting committee, the prison governor and prison medical officer. The Home Secretary accepted the findings that Ansell was sane and the execution went ahead.

On 19 July a well-behaved crowd of nearly 2,000, consisting mostly of locals, gathered outside St Albans prison. A scaffold had been built on the same spot where Thomas Wheeler was hanged in 1880. All representatives of the press were excluded. Mary Ansell walked falteringly towards the scaffold, sobbing and praying all the way there. She was heard to say, 'Oh, my God in Heaven. Lord have mercy on my soul.' She was hanged at 8 o'clock and two minutes later the crowd saw the black flag raised. Two hours later St Albans coroner Lovell Drage conducted an inquest on Ansell before her body was buried in the prison grounds.

Just seven years after the murder of Caroline Ansell a case with strange parallels took place at Leavesden Asylum. In 1906 Ernest Edward Taylor, who worked at the asylum as an engineer, died. His wife Elizabeth (a former inmate at Hill End Asylum in St Albans) was suspected of poisoning him and tried for his murder. She was found not guilty, and thus Mary Ann Ansell remains, rightly or wrongly, the last woman to be hanged in Hertfordshire.

14

A LOVE TRAGEDY

On a rainy afternoon at the beginning of June 1910, in a pretty little cottage on the banks of the River Colne, Gertrude Allen, twenty-three, was murdered by her fiancé in a sudden and unprovoked attack. The killer then calmly walked out of the house and informed the police.

Gertrude Allen lived with her father Thomas in an old cottage set among the trees in the quiet village of London Colney, five miles outside St Albans. Gertrude had been acting as housekeeper for her father since January when her mother had been taken to the county lunatic asylum at Hill End, in St Albans. Mrs Allen was due to return home the following week. Also living in the cottage was lodger Arthur Thrussell, a carter, who had come to live with the Allens at Gertrude's invitation, just after Mrs Allen's departure. He paid her ten shillings a week and shared Thomas Allen's bedroom. Thrussell and Gertrude had been seeing each other for almost three years, were said to be very much in love and were engaged to be married.

Around 5.30 a.m. on the morning of Thursday 2 June 1910 Gertrude went over to see a neighbour, Elizabeth Simmons, to tell her she would not be going to work at her job at Coursers Farm because it was too wet to work in the fields that day. She also told her that for some unknown reason Thrussell had decided not to work that day either, calling him a 'lazy hound'. She then returned home and was sitting in the kitchen with Thrussell having a cup of tea when her father left for work at 6 a.m. It was the last time he would see his daughter alive.

Elizabeth Simmons had known Gertrude since childhood and described her as a 'jolly little thing', but on this particular Thursday Gertrude seemed snappy and irritable. Elizabeth called round to the cottage about lunchtime to see if Gertrude wanted to go to Hill End Asylum that afternoon to see her mother. Elizabeth's mother was also in the asylum and she was planning a visit herself. She found Gertrude and Thrussell together in the kitchen. Thrussell was a slightly built young fellow with fair hair and complexion, blue eyes and a thin moustache. Gertrude was standing with a broom in her hand and there were dinner plates still on the table. She told Mrs Simmons that she would be going along but that Thrussell wouldn't and swore about him, saying again that if he was too lazy to go to work he was too lazy to go to the asylum. At this point Thrussell spoke up and said he simply did not wish to go. But when Elizabeth re-affirmed that Gertrude was definitely going Thrussell said, 'She don't know where she is going yet.'

Elizabeth left the cottage and returned home. About fifteen minutes later there was a knock at the door and Gertrude came in saying that she would definitely be going to the asylum and telling her friend to 'buck up and make haste'. She then went home to get changed, intending to be back shortly.

Elizabeth Simmons waited for half an hour, but Gertrude did not return, so at around 2.30 she went over to her cottage to hurry her along. She entered the kitchen but it was empty, so she went to the foot of the stairs and called 'Gertie' three times but got no answer. She was just about to mount the stairs when a male voice called down to her that Gertie would be down in a minute. Elizabeth recognised it as Thrussell's voice. She left the house and walked back over the road and had just reached her front door when a neighbour, Nellie Faulkner, called out to her, asking her, 'What's up with old Gert?' Elizabeth approached and queried why she had asked. 'Why, I heard her screaming and hollering five minutes ago, "Arthur, Arthur, don't!"' said Nellie. Elizabeth suggested perhaps they were 'larking about' as they had both been upstairs and often Gertrude would scream when they were playing around. Nellie Faulkner looked doubtful, saying it was a most unusual scream and it was the sudden silence afterwards that had frightened her. Just at that moment Thrussell emerged from the cottage, shutting the door behind him, and came towards the two women. Nellie disappeared into her house and locked the door. Thrussell leant on her windowsill and asked Elizabeth, 'Where does the policeman live?' She replied, 'Oh Arthur, what have you done to poor Gert? You ought to be ashamed of yourself.' Thrussell did not reply, just repeated the question about the policeman. He then peered into Nellie's front window saying, 'She is dead, quite dead.' Nellie almost fainted and Thrussell walked off towards PC Heard's house at Briar Cottage. He turned and saw Elizabeth about to go into the Allens' cottage and shouted out to her, 'Don't go Mrs Simmons, wait a minute.' He repeated this three times and Elizabeth retreated back home.

It was just after 2.40 p.m. and PC Heard was at home off duty when he heard a knock at his door. He answered and found Thrussell standing outside, trembling all over. Heard asked him what was the matter and Thrussell's reply was, 'I can't tell you. I have killed her.' Heard knew the Allen family well and that Gertrude and Thrussell had been courting, so therefore guessed who Thrussell meant. Heard accompanied him to the cottage and as they entered the kitchen Thrussell told the policeman, 'She is upstairs.' Heard immediately took hold of him by the arm and went upstairs into the end bedroom. Gertrude Allen was lying on the floor on her right side with her head back and her face close to the wall. Her head was in a pool of blood and there was a long, deep gash across her throat close to the mouth, almost

LOVE TRAGEDY NEAR ST. ALBANS.
YOUNG MAN CONFESSES TO KILLING HIS SWEETHEART.

The Illustrated Police News*'s reconstruction of the murder of Gertrude Allen, London Colney, 1910.*
*(*Illustrated Police News*)*

severing her head from the body. In the middle of the pool of blood was a butcher's knife with a five-inch blade. She was fully dressed with the exception of a blue skirt, which was still hanging on the bed rail. The bed was made and undisturbed. Heard took Thrussell, who made no resistance, downstairs and locked him in the kitchen. He then went out into the street and met a postman. He told him to take telegrams to Dr Smythe, the divisional surgeon, and to the police station at South Mimms.

While waiting for the police to arrive Thrussell did not talk at all, but sat in silence in the kitchen, continually smoking cigarettes.

PC Baker cycled over from South Mimms police station and examined the scene. He discovered hobnailed boot prints in the blood and, on examining Thrussell's boots, found the soles to be considerably bloodstained. His hands, especially the left, were also bloodstained. Thrussell then pointed out an extensively blood-marked towel in the scullery and a bowl containing dirty, blood-coloured water. Gertrude's father, Thomas Allen, had been fetched home from his labouring work at Gidden's farm at Colney Heath. He rushed into the kitchen and found the two policemen sitting there with Thrussell. Soon afterwards Dr Smythe arrived and pronounced Gertrude dead and her shrouded body was taken to the Bull public house opposite and placed in an adjoining barn to await the inquest. The last Thomas Allen saw of his daughter was a glimpse of her boots as she was carried out.

Thrussell was taken to Barnet police station by cab where he was charged by Inspector Brown with wilful murder. He made no reply, but began to cry. He was taken to St Albans Gaol and committed to Hertfordshire Assizes on 20 June.

Gertrude was described by all who knew her as good hearted and amicable and was generally liked. She was totally faithful to Thrussell and the two had never been known to quarrel. Thrussell was also well known in the village and was a respected character, not a drinker, and often professed how fond he was of Gertrude. Even on the day of her death, Gertrude's father noted that the couple seemed to be on happy terms when he left for work and there was no threatening or suggestion of murder. But as the coroner pointed out, 'people who commit murders do not generally tell people what they are about to do'. The motive for the murder appeared a total mystery and became the focus of village conversation for days afterwards, with groups of women flocking outside the scene, discussing the grim drama in hushed tones. During the following weekend London Colney saw an unprecedented influx of visitors to the village. Day trippers, tourists and cyclists all came to gaze upon the cottage with morbid curiosity and to watch coroner Dr Lovell Drage's arrival at the Bull at 9 a.m. on Saturday 11 June.

The deceased had a large, gaping wound in her throat about eight inches long which had caused instantaneous death. She also had bruises over her right eyebrow, below the eye and on the back of her left hand. She was discovered to be about six months pregnant. As she had no other known lover, it was assumed that the child was Thrussell's.

A curious feature of the whole affair was that Gertrude had always had a dislike of the knife that killed her. She had found it on the ground between the Bull public house and the Bull and Butcher the week before. She told a friend that she did not like the look of it because it was so big. Her father had used the knife on the morning of the murder to cut some bacon.

When summing up, the coroner stated, 'She was living in open misconduct with the man Arthur Thrussell and her language that morning was not that of a respectable woman. Even the decent, labouring poor in Hertfordshire would be ashamed of such language.'

Accordingly, a verdict of wilful murder was reached but the question of motive still haunted the proceedings. Did Thrussell kill Gertrude because she had humiliated him in front of a neighbour that Thursday lunchtime, or was it perhaps because of the child she was expecting? He appeared to have no reason to be jealous of Gertrude and why he did not go to work that day was still a mystery and a question that even he was unable to answer. At the inquest Thomas Allen was asked if the prisoner was 'madly in love' with his daughter and he replied that this was indeed the case. Appearing at the Hertford Assizes on 20 June, Thrussell was collar-less and unshaven, wearing a black jacket over a tweed waistcoat. He was pale and glanced furtively about the court. Soon the reasons for this terrible tragedy were to become clearer.

Thrussell had joined the Royal Marines in January 1906 and a month later transferred to the Royal Navy as a second-class stoker. A year later he was invalided out and sent to the Royal Naval hospital at Chatham under mental observation. At 1 a.m. on 7 January 1907 he had been seen by the quay harbourmaster to come up from the stoke hole looking 'rather queer'. When asked if he felt unwell Thrussell replied 'no' and went down below, saying, 'I will do it now.' A few minutes later the harbourmaster went to the engine room and heard a sound of somebody struggling. He found Thrussell half

Hill End, Hertfordshire's County Lunatic Asylum where Arthur Thrussell was taken after the murder of his sweetheart, Gertrude Allen. (HALS Off Acc 1025)

dazed and could get nothing out of him. Eventually Thrussell said he had tried to hang himself with his hammock ropes but could not give a reason for such an action. He appeared melancholy and answered questions in a desultory fashion.

When Thrussell's mother Sarah appeared in the witness box the prisoner's eyes welled up with tears. She told the court that several members of the family were residing in asylums and that there was a history of mental depression in the family. She also stated that he was prone to violent outbursts and could at times display extreme anger, 'looking rather wild at you'.

Dr John Lipscomb, Mayor of St Albans and Medical Officer of St Albans Gaol, had noticed that when Thrussell was first admitted he talked freely and did not seem at all upset at the crime, showing no appreciation of the severity of what he had done. At times his eyes would roll and his actions were nervy and exaggerated. Dr Lipscomb believed the violence of the act which killed his fiancée would have required maniacal force and that this pointed to insanity on the part of the accused. Another feature of insanity was that after the crime has been committed the signs of madness immediately pass away, and the very fact that Thrussell gave himself up directly afterwards was further evidence of his state of mind.

After a minute's deliberation the jury found Thrussell guilty of the act with which he was charged but that he was insane at the time. He was taken into custody as a criminal lunatic in the county asylum at Hill End, ironically the place he had refused to visit on the day of Gertrude Allen's murder.

15

THE LAST HERTFORDSHIRE HANGING

Waltham Cross, 1914

In the year 1290 Queen Eleanor, wife of King Edward I, died. Her body was brought back from Nottinghamshire for burial at Westminster. Near to each stop on the journey a monument, known as an Eleanor Cross, was erected to her memory. On 13 December the cortège spent the night at Waltham Abbey in Essex but the monument was subsequently built across the county boundary in Hertfordshire at the place now called Waltham Cross. It still stands today, albeit much renovated, and is one of just three remaining Eleanor Crosses. In 1914 another historical event took place within sight of the cross in a road named after it; a murder was committed which resulted in the last execution to take place in Hertfordshire.

Harriet Emily Whybrow was married to Joseph Whybrow, a labourer who worked at the Royal Gunpowder Factory in Waltham Abbey. They lived at 213 High Street, Waltham Cross and for the previous two years had shared the house with Harriet's stepfather George Anderson. Anderson's wife (Harriet's mother) had also lived with them until her death on 9 June 1914.

Until his wife's death George Anderson was employed as a labourer and had a reputation for being a hard worker with a short temper. Upon becoming widowed Anderson ceased to work and began drinking heavily. This led to domestic problems which came to a head on 27 June, when a drunken Anderson threatened Harriet and Joseph with an axe saying, 'I will kill the pair of you if I can get hold of you.' Joseph managed to disarm Anderson and said, 'Will you clear out of my place at once.' Anderson replied, 'No, I shan't. You can fetch forty constables and they won't take me out.' In the end Joseph fetched one policeman and Anderson left the house quietly. He spent that night sleeping in the back garden and passed the whole of the next day there. For the next two nights he slept in neighbour Emma Whitbread's outside toilet.

On Tuesday 30 June Anderson returned home once Joseph had left for work. Despite their domestic disturbances there were rumours that Anderson and Harriet were on very intimate terms and Anderson had been heard making, 'peculiar statements' about Harriet's character. Emma Whitbread proved to be something of a nosey neighbour and paid attention to what was happening next door that day. At 10 a.m. she saw Harriet and Anderson drinking beer from the same glass. Just before 1 p.m. Whitbread heard noises indicating a scuffle was taking place next door. Then she heard something bang against the wall that divided their front rooms. Whitbread went to see what was happening and saw Anderson pushing Harriet about.

At 2.15 Whitbread said she remembered hearing what she described as the sound of a knife or razor being sharpened, followed by Anderson remarking, 'That will do nicely.' By three o'clock things had calmed down. Whitbread walked past the open kitchen door of number 213 and saw Anderson and Harriet lying together face to face on a couch. They looked, 'very loving together.' This did not surprise Whitbread who had witnessed Harriet sitting on Anderson's lap several times. She later saw Harriet walking into town and Anderson following her.

At 4 p.m. Harriet Whybrow and George Anderson were in Eleanor Cross Road where a young door-to-door banana seller called Philip Rodwell saw them arguing. He witnessed Anderson draw a knife and open it behind his back. Anderson then seized Harriet by the back of her neck with his left hand and cut her throat with the knife. Harriet screamed, fell to her knees and cried out, 'Now you are satisfied you have cut my throat.' Anderson calmly closed the knife and replaced it in his pocket.

The attack had taken place in front of 130 Eleanor Cross Road, the residence of Charlotte Hicks. Hicks ran outside and upon seeing what had happened she shouted at him, 'You beast, see what you have done.' Anderson ignored her and walked off in the direction of Waltham Cross railway station. Hicks dressed Harriet's wounds as best she could and laid the stricken woman in her front garden.

In the meantime Anderson had turned round and retraced his steps up Eleanor Cross Road where he went into the Moulders' Arms pub. Before he was served, PC Walter Darlington entered the pub and arrested him. Darlington had been on duty in the vicinity of Eleanor Cross Road and was told by Philip Rodwell what had happened and where Anderson had gone. 'What have you done?' Darlington asked Anderson. He replied, 'She has been aggravating me for some time. I don't care if I hang. Is she dead?' Darlington searched Anderson and found a large wooden-handled pocket knife.

Harriet had died from a wound on the right side of her neck that had severed her jugular vein. She had bled to death before a doctor could arrive. Two policemen met Joseph Whybrow when he left work at the gunpowder factory at 5 p.m. and accompanied him to the mortuary to identify his wife's body.

Darlington took Anderson to Cheshunt police station in a cab. Detective Inspector Thomas Davis charged Anderson with Harriet's murder. His only

Waltham Cross showing the Eleanor Cross monument at the top of Eleanor Cross Road. (HALS CV Chesh/124b)

response to the charge was to sigh deeply and say, 'Oh, dear.' When police surgeon Dr W.F. Clark said to Anderson, 'This is a bad business,' Anderson was beginning to realise the magnitude of his actions. He replied, 'I don't want to think about it.'

The following day George Anderson appeared at the Cheshunt magistrates' court for committal proceedings. He appeared to be very dejected and was remanded in custody at Brixton prison for a week so that further evidence could be gathered to be presented at an adjourned sitting of the court. On the way to prison Anderson said to the police sergeant escorting him 'I wish it had never happened, sure, I shall get hung for it.' After the adjourned hearing Anderson was sent to St Albans prison to await his trial for murder at the next Hertfordshire Assizes.

Anderson stood trial for Harriet Whybrow's murder on 21 November 1914 before Judge Lawrence. When he was asked to plead Anderson responded, 'I didn't do it intentionally.' Anderson knew he could not possibly claim to be innocent of killing Harriet. Instead he tried to convince the court her death had been an accident.

Anderson gave his own account of events. He told the court that he and Harriet had drunk about five pints of beer between them at home. After leaving the house they had called in at two pubs where they had half a pint of beer at each. Harriet told Anderson that she wanted him to pawn his suit. Anderson refused and said, 'I am going to turn back if you keep on like this.' They continued walking and Anderson drew his pocket knife to cut a cake of tobacco for his pipe but Harriet kept nudging him with her elbow. 'To free himself from her attention' he swung round to get out of her way and his knife accidentally cut her throat. Anderson claimed to have no recollection of what followed until the time of his arrest.

Anderson's defence lawyer, Mr Bernard, elaborated the unlikely story. The knife was capable of inflicting the wound but it was not very sharp. This contradicted Emma Whitbread's story of hearing Anderson sharpening a knife (which Anderson denied) that suggested the murder was premeditated. Also, the act had occurred in a busy street. If Anderson had wanted to kill Harriet he could have done it undetected at home. Bernard added that Anderson had lived harmoniously with the Whybrows for over two years and that he could not remember threatening them with an axe because he had been so drunk at the time.

The trial had lasted nearly four hours. Judge Lawrence was shocked by Anderson's callousness:

Judge:	'You say this was an accident?'
Anderson:	'It was sir, a pure accident.'
Judge:	'Why did you not say so at the time?'
Anderson:	'I felt so queer. I was so cut up.'
Judge:	'Cut up! Why you walked away to a public house!'
Prosecutor:	'Why did you not stop and help this poor woman who had met with this accident?'
Anderson:	'I did not think it was so bad.'
Judge:	'Why did you not render her assistance?'
Anderson:	'She kept on pestering me.'

The judge was clearly unimpressed by Anderson whose actions after cutting Harriet's throat did not suggest that it had been an accident. He had 'left the woman to die like a dog'. After seventeen minutes of deliberation the jury found the ashen-faced Anderson guilty. The judge passed the death sentence, telling Anderson he had been found guilty on the clearest possible evidence. Anderson had killed her 'in a heartless and brutal manner, and no excuse could be found for him'.

The date for Anderson's execution was set for 8 December but this was postponed when Anderson appealed against his sentence. His appeal was to be heard at the Court of Criminal Appeal on 7 December. Anderson was not present himself but was again represented by Mr Bernard who presented his case before three judges. Bernard's attempts to save his client from the noose were disastrous. It was true that his case was terribly weak but he presented his flimsy arguments in such a long-winded and rambling manner that the judges lost patience with him.

To begin with Bernard tried to argue that the judge had summed up the case unfairly by spending an excessive time talking about the knife being sharpened. However, Judge Lawrence had pointed out at Anderson's trial that the knife was 'anything but a well-sharpened instrument'. The appeal court said, 'the learned judge at the trial appeared to have summed up the case accurately . . . in a way which could not be found fault with'.

Since Anderson's trial Bernard had discovered that Emma Whitbread had quarrelled with him in the past. Anderson had once been fined 10s for threatening her. Bernard suggested that Whitbread gave evidence against Anderson out of revenge. The judges were unimpressed, as they were when Bernard tried to argue that Philip Rodwell was an unreliable witness. Bernard's description of events was so convoluted that Mr Justice Darling said, 'the Court was really at a loss to see what the point was. Counsel [Bernard] was going on reading paragraph after paragraph. What was the point?'

The appeal court judges summed up the case in a similar fashion to the trial judge saying, 'Prisoner [Anderson] walked off to a public-house in a most absolutely callous manner quite inconsistent with the conduct of a man who, by mere accident, had cut the throat of a woman with whom he was on the ordinary terms of friendship.' Furthermore they believed that Anderson's comments when arrested were proof that he knew he had murdered her. At that time, 'The theory had not occurred to him, which he afterwards advanced, that he was cutting a piece of tobacco.' The judges were entirely unconvinced and dismissed the case saying there were 'not the slightest grounds for allowing the appeal'.

George Anderson's execution was rescheduled for 23 December at St Albans prison. Anderson was informed of the new date on 10 December. The County Surveyor tested the gallows on 16 December and found they were in perfect working order. William Willis from Manchester wrote to St Albans prison offering his services as executioner. Willis had assisted hangman John Ellis at the previous execution at St Albans, that of Charles Coleman in 1911.[†] He was turned down in favour of John Ellis whom the High Sheriff of Hertfordshire, whose duty it was to arrange executions, considered to be 'a

---

† Charles Coleman had stabbed to death Rose Ann Gurney in Rickmansworth Park on 15 July 1911. Coleman had a long list of previous convictions for such offences as indecent behaviour in a church, larceny, wilful damage, game trespass, assault, drunk and disorderly and attempted murder. On the day he murdered Gurney he had just been released from prison after serving a six-month sentence for mutilating a dog. He was executed on 21 December 1911.

LIST OF CANDIDATES REPORTED TO BE COMPETENT FOR THE OFFICE OF EXECUTIONER, OR WHO HAVE ACTED AS ASSISTANTS AT EXECUTIONS.

NAME AND ADDRESS.	REMARKS.
JOHN ELLIS, 320 ~~100~~, Oldham Road, Rochdale.	Has satisfactorily conducted executions, has assisted at executions, and has been practically trained at Newgate Prison.
THOMAS W. PIERREPOINT, Town End, Clayton, Near Bradford, Yorkshire.	Has satisfactorily conducted executions, has assisted at executions, and has been practically trained at Pentonville Prison.
WILLIAM WILLIS, 22, Bunyan Street, Hyde Road, Ardwick, Manchester.	Has assisted at executions, and has been practically trained at Pentonville Prison.
~~ALBERT F. LUMB,~~ ~~100, Hartington Terrace,~~ ~~Lidget Green,~~ ~~Bradford, Yorks.~~ 2 Mayville Road, St Peters Kent.	~~Has assisted at executions, and has been practically trained at Pentonville Prison.~~
GEORGE BROWN, ~~55, Trafalgar Street,~~ ~~Ashton-under-Lyne.~~ 39 Clarendon Road, Broadstairs Kent	Has assisted at executions, and has been practically trained at Pentonville Prison.

x (33)20090 Pk 42 100 12/13 E & S

The Home Office's list of candidates to execute George Anderson. Ellis was given the job and was assisted by Brown. (HALS SH2/4/2/33)

very competent and experienced man'. Ellis had executed Dr Crippen in 1910. George Brown of Kent was employed as assistant to Ellis.

It had been ninety years since a crowd of 15,000 had assembled in Hertford for the execution of John Thurtell. The execution of George Anderson could not have been more different. Perhaps the populace were more concerned with the outbreak of war but remarkably, with the exception of a handful of soldiers billeted in St Albans, nobody gathered outside the gaol at eight o'clock on that raw and foggy morning.

The execution went ahead without incident and the death bell tolled for fifteen minutes from the tower of St Paul's church. Anderson's body was left hanging for an hour before being taken down and subjected to a coroner's inquest. Ellis and Brown were seen leaving the prison at 8.20, each carrying a black bag and smoking a cigar. Hertfordshire had seen its last execution.

16

THE SHOP MURDER
MYSTERY

Hitchin, 1919

The murder of Hitchin shopkeeper Elizabeth Ridgley and her pet dog Prince in 1919 remains officially unsolved to this day. It was described by the veteran crime journalist Norman Hastings as 'one of the most remarkable in the annals of crime and would provide a good foundation for a detective novel'.

In about the year 1910 William Ridgley and his wife Elizabeth moved from their shop in Baldock Road, Letchworth and opened a small shop at 125 Nightingale Road, Hitchin that stocked a remarkably large range of goods including cigarettes, vegetables, flour, sugar, tea, tinned food, earthenware and toys. When William died in December 1917 Elizabeth ran the shop alone with her Irish terrier Prince for company. The dog had a gentle nature but was well known for his hostility towards strangers.

Elizabeth and Prince survived a fire in the shop in May 1918 but otherwise business continued normally. The shop was situated on a busy thoroughfare between the town centre and the railway station. Ridgley used the shop's income for buying stock and paying her bills. She never kept more than a week's takings on the premises but did have a collection of 350 three-penny pieces in a chest in her bedroom.

On Saturday 25 January 1919 Annie Withey who lived at 121 Nightingale Road saw Ridgley at her gate and spoke to her at 8.30 p.m.. Ernest Rutland lived opposite Mrs Ridgley at no. 46. He was returning from the cinema at 8.58 when he saw the shop door open and the light on. He went up the road to the fried fish shop, returning at around 9.07. The shop door was now closed but the light was still on.

Ridgley's neighbour at 126 Nightingale Road was Louisa Roach. Their kitchens adjoined each other and were separated by a thin wall. Sometime after 8.20 p.m. Roach heard Prince barking furiously but thought nothing of it as the dog always barked at strangers. Roach then heard a loud thud from which she drew the bizarre conclusion that Ridgley had killed her pet.

By 11.15 that night Roach was in bed. She heard loud groaning and moaning coming from Ridgley's house which continued until one or two o'clock the next morning. Again Roach was unconcerned. She thought it might have been one of the soldiers who were billeted at no. 124 with Mr and Mrs Wheeler suffering from toothache. Mrs Wheeler was hearing things herself. At 1.30 a.m. she heard a thud which she thought was a soldier falling out of bed, but she checked and found it wasn't.

On Monday morning customer Gertrude Day called at the shop but found the door locked. She returned later but the door was still locked. Day went round the back of the shop and saw the back door was ajar. She did not try to enter and investigate as she was afraid of the dog. Something was obviously wrong and she sent for the police. PC Kirby arrived, climbed over the locked back gate and went through the back door. He found Elizabeth Ridgley lying face down on the floor across the doorway between the hall and living room. The dead body of Prince was lying about a yard away. Nearby he saw a four pound weight covered in blood and hair, both human and dog.

Kirby sent for Dr William Grellett, a surgeon at Hitchin hospital who also acted as a police surgeon. Grellett observed injuries on Ridgley's head which he thought were caused by a blunt instrument. She had been dead for over eight hours. Grellett said that 'The whole place was covered with blood' and noted blood on the shop counter. There was an empty bloodstained cash box by Ridgley's body.

Superintendent George Reed from Hitchin police station arrived at the shop after Ridgley's corpse had been taken to the mortuary. After examining the scene by candlelight Reed came to the astonishing conclusion that Ridgley had killed her dog and then died after accidentally falling on a pile of crockery and saucepan handles which were covered in blood. He then allowed Ridgley's sister to open the shop in the first week of February and a stream of customers entered the shop, possibly destroying clues. Ridgley herself was buried on 1 February at Hitchin cemetery.

Hertfordshire's appropriately named Chief Constable Alfred Letchworth Law was not convinced by Reed's conclusions. On 5 February Law called in Scotland Yard to take over the investigation. Chief Inspector Frederick Wensley arrived in Hitchin the next day. He visited the shop and, 'Having gone carefully over the place, I found it impossible to accept his [Reed's] theory of accidental death or the deductions by which he arrived at it.'

Reed's unusual solution to Elizabeth Ridgley's death was not the only thing which caused friction between the Hitchin Division of the Hertfordshire Constabulary and Scotland Yard. Wensley later reported:

The conditions under which we did our duty for several weeks at Hitchin were exceedingly bad. The weather was bitterly cold, we did not expect neither did we receive any sympathetic assistance from Supt. Reed. We were compelled to use a room in the house where the murder was committed as an office, the stench, at times, was almost unendurable,

The Illustrated Police News's *reconstruction of the discovery of the bodies of Elizabeth Ridgley and her dog Prince. (*Illustrated Police News)

this together with the long hours daily performed for weeks was a very severe test of physical endurance.

Home Office pathologist Dr Bernard Spilsbury was called to examine the medical evidence. Spilsbury had first made a name for himself when he had given evidence at the trial of Dr Crippen in 1910. Since then he had appeared at many high-profile murder trials. Ridgley's coffin was exhumed and taken to the mortuary at Hitchin hospital where Spilsbury conducted a post-mortem. He also made an examination of Prince's head.

Spilsbury concluded that Ridgley had died from meningeal haemorrhage consequent to fractures of her skull. The fractures could not have been caused by hitting the back of her head as Reed had suggested. They were the result of 'blows delivered by another person'. A blunt weapon such as a poker or one of the edges of the four pound weight had been used with considerable force. The pathologist deduced that Ridgley must have been lying face downwards when most or perhaps all of the blows were delivered from different angles. Ridgley's hands and arms were bruised, suggesting she had tried to protect herself before the fatal blows were struck.

Spilsbury added that death would not have occurred until hours after the attack. Ridgley would have been unconscious for a while from shock before partially regaining consciousness until she died. It appears that Louisa Roach had heard her neighbour being attacked after eight, regaining consciousness by one o'clock and dying later. After studying Spilsbury's report and taking statements, Wensley wrote a report laying out what he thought had happened on 25 January:

That the back door of No. 125, Nightingale Road, on the night of 25th January, was locked and bolted by the deceased and the small lamp lit in the scullery as usual.

That the 4 lb. weight was in its usual place by the scale in the kitchen on that date.

That robbery was the motive.

That the assailant was probably a casual customer and knew little or nothing of the interior of the premises.

That he was a local man as it would have been very difficult for him to have left the district after committing the crime, owing to the fact that there were no main line trains running after the approximate time of the crime.

That he entered the shop by the street door shortly after 8.30 p.m. and probably caused the deceased to go into the rear of the premises to fetch something in order that he might rob the till, but finding that he could not open the till drawer from the customers side of the counter, as it was kept in position by a catch, he went into the passage, met the deceased and perhaps the dog and attacked them both with some blunt instrument.

That the assailant was probably injured himself by the dog, most likely bitten on the hands, hence the drops of blood on the counter and the till drawer.

That the first attack was probably delivered at the living room door, where most of the blood was found.

That most likely the deceased and dog were dazed and felled at the first onslaught.

That the assailant then robbed the till, bolted the front street door, found the weight in the scullery and either through fear or frenzy, perhaps both, hammered them about the head with it while they lay on the ground.

That there was some screaming by the deceased and whining of the dog.

That it was heard by Mrs. Roach and her family and she showed a regrettable indifference, amounting to callousness.

That the assailant left by the back entrance with the contents of the till which represented the day's takings.

On 15 February Inspector Wensley arrested Irish labourer John Healy who had been seen loitering outside Ridgley's shop on the night of the murder and had returned home unusually late. Healy was thirty-three years old and a former soldier. He had lived in Hitchin with his wife since August 1918. At the time of his arrest he was lodging at 16 Radcliffe Road which was 200 yards away from Ridgley's house.

Healy was taken to Hitchin police station where he made a statement. He said that on 25 January he had visited the Plough and Dial pub in Hitchin and left there between 8 and 9 p.m. He could not recall what time he returned home but he thought he had returned straight home from the pub (the police later estimated this would have taken him 13½ minutes). He had twice previously made purchases at Ridgley's shop but had not been in there for months. Healy said that a scar on the first finger of his right hand was caused by an accident at the Kryn Lahy factory in Letchworth where he started working the week after Ridgley's death. He denied having bought any new clothes since 25 January.

Wensley detained Healy in custody while he investigated his statement. Two days later Healy was charged with Ridgley's murder. He responded to the charge by saying, 'I know nothing about it, that's all.' The next day Healy made his first of five appearances before the magistrate. The hearings were repeatedly adjourned while Wensley accumulated his evidence that was gradually presented.

Details of the search of Healy's room were given. Several bloodstained articles were found including the top portion of a pair of Healy's trousers. It was implied that the missing portion might have been bloodstained and torn by a dog's teeth. Healy's clothes were taken from him at the police station for examination. Several items were bloodstained and it had been noticed that Healy had cuts on his right hand which could have been caused by a dog bite.

Mavis Smith, the young daughter of Healy's landlady, recalled seeing Healy on the night of the murder. He was standing at the corner by Ridgley's shop at around 8.20 p.m. She added that Healy usually returned home at 9 p.m. unless he had been to the cinema. On the night of Ridgley's murder Healy had returned via the side door at 10.30 and gone straight to bed. He came downstairs the next morning at eleven o'clock with a bandaged finger. Fellow lodger Jens Christian Christiansen told an identical story. Mavis said that Healy had shown her a new shirt he had bought on 27 January. When she asked Healy's wife why her husband's finger was bandaged she was told that Healy had fallen off a chair when drunk.

William Augustus Craswell, a Hitchin tailor, identified Healy as a man he had seen in Ridgley's shop at around 8.15 p.m. on the night of her murder buying tobacco and matches. It also emerged that Healy had left his job on 24 January complaining of insufficient wages. At the time of Ridgley's death he owed his landlady 24s back rent which he paid two days after the murder.

Despite his time in custody and a murder charge hanging over him, Healy did not appear to be feeling any pressure. Throughout the hearings he took notes and occasionally smiled at the witnesses' statements. His landlady Annie Smith recalled that on 25 January Healy had gone out alone at around 7 p.m. and returned home and gone straight to bed, forsaking his customary cup of cocoa or Bovril. The next day she noticed he had a rag tied round the first finger of his right hand. She asked, 'Jack, what is the matter with your finger?' He replied, 'I've knocked it.' There was no record of Healy injuring his hand in the accident book at Kryn Lahy where Healy said the injury had occurred.

There was some evidence in Healy's favour. On Christmas Eve 1918 a fellow lodger had returned to Radcliffe Road bleeding heavily from a cut in his head. Healy had helped him upstairs and had possibly got some of his blood on his clothing.

Healy was finally committed to trial at the Assizes on 18 March. His solicitor George Passingham protested. He said that his client had no motive to kill Ridgley. There was no question of a quarrel, revenge or robbery. Healy did have £6 3s on him when he was arrested but this was from a war gratuity of £8 10s he received on 31 December.

Chief Constable Law wrote to the Metropolitan Police Commissioner to praise Wensley's handling of the investigation. Law knew of the difficulties the Scotland Yard man had encountered and wrote, 'the case required considerable tact and perspicacity in order to bring it to a successful issue and to avoid friction with the local officers'. Superintendent Reed retired at the end of April after thirty-three years' service. This was unconnected to his ignominious involvement in the Ridgley investigation. He had planned to retire in 1917 but stayed on because of the war. He took a new job with Healy's employers Kryn Lahy.

3 IN THE *County* OF *Hertford*
PETTY SESSIONAL DIVISION OF *Hitchin*

Register of the Court of Summary Jurisdiction, *sitting at*

Number	Name of Informant or Complainant	Name of Defendant	Age of Defendant, if known	Nature of Offence, or of Matter of Complaint	Date of Offence
1	2	3		4	5
(43)	Chief Inspector Wensley.	John Healy	33	Feloniously wilfully and of his malice aforethought did kill and murder one Elizabeth Ridgeley.	25 Jan 1919.
44	Beatrice Eliza Farrow	Frederick Claud Farrow.		application for a Separation order on the ground of persistent cruelty	
45	James Ayrmedove	Elizabeth King George 12		School Bye Laws	
46		Alice Worsley			
47		Mary Louisa Bray Alfred 13 Rose Bray 10			

Entry in the Hitchin magistrates' court register for one of Healy's five appearances there. (HALS PS 12/1/25)

The trial of John Healy took place in June 1919 at the Hertford Assizes. It was described by a local newspaper as 'probably the most remarkable with which the town of Hitchin is ever likely to be associated'. Because of the hot weather the court windows were left half-open and during tense moments during the proceedings the laughter of children and the hum of the gathered crowd outside could be heard.

The charismatic Sir Edward Marshall Hall led the prosecution. Hall immediately dismissed Reed's initial theory which he described as 'the view formed by a member of the Police Force at Hitchin, who has now retired. . . . I cannot understand how a theory of accidental death could have prevailed in the mind of anybody of experience in such matters.' The court universally rejected Reed's theory. Judge Darling agreed that 'only the police' held that theory. Darling was scathing of the local police's initial investigation throughout the trial. He later commented, 'Every precaution seems to have been taken in the early days to ensure that nobody should be detected.' Cecil Hayes, acting for Healy's defence, quickly pointed out that he would not be using it in defence of Healy. He would instead be putting a good deal of reliance on Healy's previous good character.

Hall stated that the medical evidence pointed to the fact that Elizabeth Ridgley had been murdered and that he wanted to address three points from Healy's statement to Inspector Wensley.

1 – Healy claimed that injuries on his right thumb and first finger had been received at Kryn Lahy's. This was at odds with the statements of those who had seen it on 26 January, before Healy had started working there.

2 – Healy claimed that he had not bought or been given any new clothes prior to his interview with Wensley on 15 February. However, Healy was wearing a pair of trousers that had never been washed and it could be proved he had bought a new shirt on 27 January.

3 – Healy claimed that he had not been into Mrs Ridgley's shop for months but there was a witness who claimed to have seen Healy in the shop on the night of the crime.

Hall then told the jury what he thought had happened on the night of Ridgley's murder:

Whoever got into the house in all probability got in at the front door. That door was open a few minutes before nine; it was shut at ten minutes past nine. The man probably secreted himself in the house until the woman could shut up the shop. She had gone into the back room. I suggest to you that there was some discussion between the assailant and the dead woman – something amounting to an altercation. And at that moment the dog interfered. It made for the assailant. He endeavoured to get hold of the dog, and in trying to collar the animal it bit his hand. The man thereupon – this is the theory of the prosecution – seizes the weight, and with it he goes to strike the dog. The woman, fond of her dog – as women are – now interferes again, with a view to protecting the dog. The man then strikes her on the back of the head and knocks her senseless. Having done that – he has killed the dog by a very lucky blow, for the skulls of dogs are very thick – he bashes the woman on the head with the weight while she was lying there, thus causing the four tremendous wounds on the back of the head which caused her death. He drags the body partly out of the room – by the hair of the head – and then he goes to the till to see if he can find any money there. Then, having extinguished any light there was, he makes his escape by the back door.

Bernard Spilsbury caused a stir when he gave evidence by producing a human skull and placing it on the handrail of the witness stand. Some observers thought at first it was Ridgley's skull but it was only a prop to illustrate where the blows had struck Ridgley.

There were further dramatics when Hall asked Healy to grasp the four pound shop weight in his hand which he did without hesitation. This effectively put the murder weapon in the hands of the prime suspect. Hall asked Healy to exhibit how he would use such a weight against a dog attacking him. Healy coolly replied that his preferred method would be to throw the weight at the dog.

Healy gave an account of his movements on the night of the murder. His story was clearly at odds with the evidence given by his landlady and her daughter. Healy said that on 25 January he stayed in the Plough and Dial until nearly 9 p.m. He returned home around 9 p.m. sat down in the dining room, had some supper, read a paper and talked to the other people there before going to bed. He denied there was a rag on his finger on the 26th and said he had injured his finger on the 28th while loading trucks at work.

Healy had maintained a cool demeanour so far but this began to crack under cross-examination. Hall asked about Craswell's statement that he had seen Healy in Ridgley's shop on 25 January. Healy said that Craswell was 'absolutely wrong'. Hall asked, 'Do you say he has invented it or made a mistake?' Healy angrily replied, 'Either Craswell or me is telling lies, and may Almighty God strike the liar dead!'

The prisoner later suggested that he was the innocent victim of a plot because of an incident in connection with a fellow lodger's money that happened at Christmas. The Smiths wanted 'to banish him from the town of Hitchin'. Hall asked if he really believed that the Smiths had invented evidence to get him convicted. Healy replied, 'It is to get me away from the town of Hitchin at any rate.'

When questioned by his defence, Healy's answers were unconvincing. He said that one of the bloodstained shirts was just an undershirt and he could not explain the presence of bloodstains on it. Then he denied ever having a wound on his right thumb. As this contradicted Dr Grellett's evidence Judge Darling ordered Spilsbury to examine Healy's right hand. Spilsbury observed a nodule indicating a former injury.

Hall summed up the case for the prosecution for an hour, emphasising the weight of the testimony contradicting Healy's account of his movements on 25 January. Hayes addressed the jury for twice as long, stressing the absence of bloodstains on Healy's outer clothing and suggesting the prosecution witnesses had all mistaken the date they had said was 25 January.

In his summing up the judge was very critical of the way the case was initially handled. He thought Reed's theory that Ridgley had killed her dog and then committed suicide 'was absurd' and that he had 'apparently endeavoured to obtain material to support his theory which was a very dangerous thing to do'. This had resulted in time being wasted and clues destroyed.

Darling told the jury they had to give Healy the benefit of the doubt and reminded them there was no 'Not Proven' verdict in English law. He added that 'it did not follow that because a verdict of 'Not Guilty' was returned it necessarily followed that the prisoner was innocent but merely that his guilt had not been established to their satisfaction beyond any reasonable doubt.' He regretted that a signed statement by Healy's wife which was in the hands of the prosecution could not be used as the Crown could not compel her to give evidence against her husband. The statement said that she was at home on the night of 25 January when Healy returned and could have provided crucial evidence as to what time he had returned.

After considering their verdict for ten minutes the jury returned to declare Healy 'not guilty'. He left the court by a side exit and went off in the direction of Port Vale with his wife who had been waiting outside the court. No. 125 Nightingale Road was soon reoccupied and the case remained unsolved.

Chief Inspector Frederick Wensley. Wensley was convinced John Healy had got away with murder. (Stewart P. Evans)

However, an angry Wensley had other ideas. He knew the contents of the statement made by Healy's wife. She said he had returned home at 10 p.m., an hour later than Healy had said. His finger was cut then, not the next week as Healy had said. She made a later statement admitting to binding Healy's finger with a piece of rag on 26 January. Healy had said he had bound it himself with a piece of rag he had in his pocket. Healy slept on the right side of their bed where bloodstains were found. She added that Healy's mother had shown signs of insanity and her husband 'was sometimes strange in his manner'. In his report in the Scotland Yard files Wensley reflected on what might have been:

I have no hesitation in saying that Healy committed this murder and I am certain that had we been earlier on the scene we should have obtained more definite evidence of his guilt. I think it is reasonable to assume that many articles in the shop and parlour were handled by the assailant and had ordinary care been exercised we should most probably have obtained some excellent finger impressions which would have placed beyond the possibility of a doubt the prisoner's guilt. Unfortunately before we arrived every trace in this direction had been obliterated and cleaned. In addition to this the publicity given to Supt. Reed's theory of suicide prevented people who did eventually render us most valuable assistance, from coming forward as they would undoubtedly have done at a very much earlier stage had there been no doubt thrown upon the cause of the death of Mrs. Ridgley.

17

A 'RUM AFFAIR'

In the early hours of the morning on 28 January 1921 the phone rang in the Criminal Investigation Department of New Scotland Yard. It was the Deputy Chief Constable of Hertfordshire Constabulary asking for assistance in a case of suspected murder at the quiet village of Redbourn.

Sergeant Askew and Inspector Crutchet proceeded immediately from London to the county police station in St Albans where they were briefed on the facts of the case. A seventy-one-year-old woman named Sarah Seabrook had died in suspicious circumstances. Her daughter, Mrs Jessie Freeman, twenty-six, had been the first on the scene and was waiting anxiously at the police station. The officers took the opportunity of taking a detailed statement from her.

Sarah Seabrook had been widowed for eleven years when she died on 27 January 1921. Born Sarah Chalkley on 9 July 1850, she had lived in the small two-up, two-down cottage at 6 Redbourn Common for over sixty years. She had given birth to all her ten children there and her husband Charles Abel had also passed away in the cottage. She now shared it with three of her children, her eldest son Herbert, forty-six, and spinsters May, thirty-five, and Olive, thirty-two. Jessie lived with her husband in the High Street. Since 1919 Sarah had suffered two apoplectic seizures and the family was warned by the local doctor not to leave their mother alone longer than was absolutely necessary. Between themselves they organised a finely tuned routine so that Sarah was only alone for around an hour each day except on two afternoons between 2 and 3.30, at which time it was customary for her to have a nap.

On the day her mother died Jessie had needed to go to the neighbouring town of Harpenden in the afternoon and had left just after 1 p.m. when her sister May returned to the cottage for her lunch break. Her mother kissed her goodbye as usual and both she and May waved her off at the gate. Jessie rode the short distance into Harpenden on her bike.

During the preceding few weeks small sums of money had gone missing from the house. On one occasion half a crown had disappeared from the mantelpiece and a florin from May's handbag on the front room table. About a week before Sarah's death some more money had unaccountably gone astray. The family resolved to ensure that their mother bolted both front and back doors and put the key on the inside windowsill whenever she was left alone.

Jessie returned from Harpenden at 3.30 and discovered the house full of smoke. Assuming her mother was still resting upstairs, she rushed into the kitchen to find a chair was on fire. Several items of clothing that had been airing in front of the fire now lay in ashes in the grate.

With her gloved hands Jessie attempted to put out the flames then flung open the kitchen door to let the smoke out and threw the chair into the back garden. As she came back inside she became aware of a strange gurgling noise which appeared to come from between the doorpost and the sink. As the smoke cleared she saw her mother lying on the floor with her back against the wall, her face covered with blood. Her right arm was resting over a pail of water and her head was leaning on her arm and the blood trickled into the water. Jessie repeatedly asked her mother what she had done to herself, but Sarah was unable to make any coherent statement. Thick bubbles of blood came from her mouth when she tried to speak and all Jessie could make out were the words 'Jessie, Jessie'.

Thinking her mother had suffered another seizure and may have fallen on the fire, Jessie ran to Mrs Litton, the next-door neighbour but one, to seek help. All she found was the thirteen-year-old son, Donald, standing in the kitchen in nothing but his shirt, who told her that his mother was out. Jessie then ran to a nearby house and called for the family friend Mr Bradshaw, shouting, 'Come quickly, mother is burning, Walt.' Bradshaw was joined by two other neighbours and the three of them carried Sarah into the back garden and put her in an armchair. It was then Jessie noticed something very odd about the poker lying beside the fire. It was bent into the shape of a half moon, whereas it had been perfectly straight when she stirred the fire earlier in the day.

Outside, a group of curious schoolchildren was beginning to gather as neighbours rushed in and out of the cottage. In an attempt to stem the bleeding, towels and a sheet were wrapped around Sarah's head and a wound on her thumb was bandaged. Bradshaw was telling her to spit the blood out and he faintly heard her mutter 'oh dear, oh dear'. The blood was thick and dark and appeared to be choking her. He ordered Jessie to get the doctor, but she fell into a state of collapse, so the young son of the landlord of the Red Lion pub volunteered to go. He was soon back saying the doctor was out on calls and was not expected to return for some while. Bradshaw took Jessie's bike and rode to the house of the district nurse, Angela Moore, nearby.

Meanwhile, May Seabrook had been fetched home from work. She rushed into the back garden and, on seeing the condition of her mother, screamed and fell into a neighbour's arms. Amid all the chaos Nurse Moore arrived, expecting to find the victim of a stroke but, on removing the sheet, she found deep gashes on Sarah's forehead and temples but no evidence to suggest she had burnt herself. She wondered if Sarah had momentarily lost her reason and cut herself about. She advised the old woman be removed to hospital

How Sarah Seabrook was found, with terrible head injuries, in her cottage in Redbourn, 1921. (Illustrated Police News)

immediately. St Albans hospital was full but a bed was secured at West Herts Hospital at Hemel Hempstead some five miles away.

Bradshaw borrowed a car from the local garage and called to some male neighbours to help carry Sarah to the car. By now the word had spread that something had happened to old Mrs Seabrook and the villagers gathered outside to watch as Nurse Moore, the widow's daughter-in-law and Bradshaw took Sarah off to hospital. Jessie wanted to accompany them but she wasn't allowed, being too upset. Olive and Jessie's husband then arrived and the neighbours told them to go to Mrs Bradshaw's for tea and not to go back into the house until it was cleared up and fit for them to see.

Sarah's second youngest son, Ethelbert, was riding his bicycle home from work when he met the car taking his mother to the hospital and followed it there. On the journey Sarah was very agitated and restless. She seemed to be trying to push someone away and was saying, 'Let me get up' and 'Don't let him touch me', and something else that they could not understand.

On arrival at the hospital Sarah was examined by Dr Georgina Davidson who gave little hope of recovery and advised the relatives to attend as speedily as possible. But she was not convinced about the seizure theory, saying 'The condition of the woman made me very suspicious that something out of the ordinary had happened to her.' Ethelbert went close to the bed and called 'mother' three times but her eyes remained closed and she made no response. Sarah was bleeding continually from the nose, ears and mouth and finally died at 5.55 p.m.

The hospital reported the death to the police in Hemel Hempstead at about 7.30 that night and Inspector Pryor from St Albans and PC Hunt from Redbourn went to the cottage to investigate. Unfortunately, believing that Sarah had had another seizure and her injuries were caused by her falling about, well-meaning friends and neighbours had cleared up most of the blood in the cottage and the only evidence of anything untoward was the mysteriously bent poker. The only person who inspected the house following the accident was Nurse Moore and she told the police that as she had walked through the kitchen she noticed blood on an upturned enamel bowl in the sink and also on the window ledge just above the sink. When she had attended to Sarah's wounds, she had asked May if she might see the room where her mother slept. Both upstairs rooms were still full of smoke. Sarah's single bed bore an indentation as if someone had been lying down. There was also a double bed in the room, apparently occupied by the two spinster daughters. A table was overturned and the window curtain was torn. Blood was everywhere – on the floor beneath the window, beside the bed, on the ironwork of the bed and on the corner of a sheet near the foot. On the landing outside the front bedroom there were marks as if someone had stepped in blood without shoes, walked across the landing and down the stairs. Nurse Moore remembered that Sarah had been without shoes when she saw her. Going downstairs, she noticed there was also blood on the sleeve of a coat hanging on a nail at the bottom of the stairs.

Jessie had told the nurse that she had often asked her mother what she would do if she had another seizure while alone in the house and Sarah had said that she would crawl to the window to attract attention and the torn curtain in the bedroom seemed to suggest this is what had happened. A teetotaller, Sarah had often suffered violent shooting pains in the head since her seizures had begun. A fortnight before her death, Jessie stated that the pain had caused Sarah to call out 'Oh!' and clutch the mantelpiece. She said, 'Mother had not been able to bend forward for months and my sister would put her shoes on for her. But in the days before her death she had said she felt better than she had for months, that the headaches were not so bad and her head felt clearer.'

At midnight more police officers visited the cottage on Redbourn Common and on finding the bent poker, began to suspect foul play. There was much activity in this normally peaceful neighbourhood, with police cars coming and going late into the night. Then at 4 a.m. the call to New Scotland Yard was placed.

Sergeant Askew and Inspector Crutchet came to Redbourn and secured accommodation at the Bull Hotel. They then went to the scene of the crime before attending the inquest on the deceased at 5 p.m. Later that evening, they saw the body in the mortuary and were both of the opinion that the severe head injuries were unlikely to have been caused by Sarah falling about trying to attract attention. Crutchet asked for the Home Office pathologist, Dr Bernard Spilsbury, to carry out a post-mortem. The following day, 29 January, Dr Spilsbury arrived in Redbourn and looked around the cottage before travelling to West Herts hospital to carry out the post-mortem.

Sarah Seabrook had sustained twenty-eight distinct blows and wounds to the head, four impressed fractures of the skull, her left ear had been cut into strips and her left forearm was fractured and extensively bruised. Spilsbury noted that she had an exceptionally thick skull for her age, otherwise her head would have been smashed to a pulp. Later that night Spilsbury returned to Redbourn police station where he was shown the bent poker and confirmed it was a weapon such as would cause the injuries he had found.

An event that had originally been looked upon as an unusual accident was suddenly viewed as a brutal and savage attack on a vulnerable old woman and Redbourn leapt into national prominence with everyone wanting to know who killed Mrs Seabrook. The police were calling it a 'rum affair' and the villagers were horrified; surely no one in their community could have committed such an atrocious crime. It must be an opportunist. Children were playing on the common outside at around the time of the attack, but no strangers had been seen in the area. Mr Bradshaw, who lived nearby, confirmed that he had been working at his front gate all day and had seen no one suspicious. Yet a few miles away in Totteridge another woman was battered around the head in a vicious attack on the same day. Were the two crimes connected?

The police now felt certain they were looking for a murderer and Askew and Crutchet returned to the cottage. Because of the neighbours' well-intentioned clean-up there was little to go on. There were no footprints in the house, but the two policemen discovered the print of a hobnailed boot at the side of a rainwater tank in the back garden beneath the kitchen window. They covered it with a bowl until such time as they could obtain a plaster cast of it.

The members of the Seabrook family who lived at the cottage joined the police and it was ascertained that nothing had been stolen, making the motive for the attack unclear. However, £14 and four ten-shilling notes were discovered in a locked chest of drawers near Sarah's bed. The family claimed to have had no idea that she had savings of such an amount.

The following day, 1 February, the police continued their investigations in the village. They questioned thirteen-year-old Donald Litton, whose house Jessie Freeman had first come to after discovering her injured mother. When the police enquired as to why he had not been attending school that day, Litton replied that the afternoon before he had fallen over in the playground and badly cut his knee. He told them that on the 27th his mother had gone out at two o'clock and about a quarter of an hour later he had gone out to draw some water from the well that served the three cottages, about two or three yards from the Seabrook house. As he stood on the woodwork of the well he forgot about his stiff, bandaged knee and slipped in. He grabbed at the chain, but it slipped through his hands and he slid down into the water but, managing to keep his head above the water level, he clambered back up by pressing his feet and back against the opposite walls of the well and pressing his hands on the bricks underneath him. He believed he must have inched his way to the top of the well by about half past two. He went straight home and took his clothes off, throwing them into a bath with his boots. He then sat in front of the fire, reading, with nothing but his shirt on, until his mother returned at around 5 p.m. He told her what had happened and that he had heard something had happened to Mrs Seabrook and she should go and find out. He told the police that he knew the deceased very well and had been to her house on several occasions to ask the time when their clock had stopped or when Jessie Freeman had brought shopping back for them. He had often fetched water for the old woman in return.

But the police were suspicious. If Litton's story were true, they felt it would have been a 'remarkable coincidence that in the short space of time left between his getting out of the well and the deceased being found a stranger should have gained access to the back of the house, secured admittance, of which there was no sign of forcible entry, and inflicted the serious and numerous wounds on the deceased without being seen or heard'. However, when questioned, Charles Henry Ford, a lodger at the Littons' house, who was working at Redbournbury Farm on the day of the murder, confirmed that Donald's story was the same one he had told both himself and his mother, and that he himself had fetched up the boy's cap from the well the following day.

The police then closely questioned George Freeman, husband of Jessie, about his wife's visit to Harpenden on the afternoon of the murder, she having told them that she went in order to deliver a message to her husband concerning an order for a gatepost. Freeman's answers were vague and he looked uncomfortable throughout the questioning. Suspicions were raised and the police resolved to investigate further.

When asked to produce the clothing she was wearing when she found her mother, Jessie handed over the dress and boots but said she had taken the coat to St Albans to be dyed black. The police tried to obtain it but it had already been through the dyeing process.

Later Freeman returned and said he had something to confess. Jessie had lied about the purpose of her visit to Harpenden and he had felt obliged to cover up for her in his interview. She had no message to deliver about a gatepost, but had merely gone into the village to do some shopping. She thought that if she had told the police this she would have been heavily criticised by both them and neighbours for leaving her mother alone for such a trivial matter as shopping.

Jessie was called back in for interview and this time gave a true statement, which was borne out by witnesses, and she was cleared. When asked if she knew of anyone who bore her late mother any ill will, Jessie replied that Sarah had never got along with her immediate neighbours at number seven. These were the Misses Weston, two elderly 'maiden ladies', one of whom was an invalid. Disagreements began over the use of the shared lavatory and then worsened in 1918 when Jessie was constantly playing the piano before a music exam. She told police her mother had not spoken to them for three years or more. The only interest the elderly Miss Emma Weston had taken on the day of the murder was enquiring of a neighbour, 'Is the house on fire?' Being reassured that it wasn't, she simply went back inside and shut the door.

Next to be investigated was Herbert Seabrook, the eldest son and a farm labourer at Harpendenbury Farm. Herbert was single and lived at home with his mother and sisters and was described as being 'deaf and somewhat dull in intellect'. His movements were also borne out by witnesses and he was not questioned further.

Then one suspicious fact came to light. It appeared Sarah had misgivings about who had been responsible for the missing money. On the evening of Tuesday 25 January Sarah, May, Jessie and her husband were having dinner at the cottage. Sarah told them that that afternoon she had gone into the garden and had seen Donald Litton in his garden. After a minute he disappeared and, as she went back inside through the back door, she was surprised to see him walk in the front door. She had said, 'Hello Donald, what do you want, to know the time?' When he replied that he did, she said, 'The clock is twenty minutes to one but it is ten minutes fast.' Donald had then walked straight through the house. Sarah told her family, 'the little brat walked straight through the house and shut the door up, a thing he had never done before'.

Inspector Crutchet went to Mrs Litton and asked if her son had worn his boots since the day he fell down the well. She replied that he had not, and the policeman took them away, along with the clothes he had been wearing, to show Dr Spilsbury. When the imprints matched exactly the cast that had been taken from outside Sarah Seabrook's kitchen window, Crutchet sent Sergeants Askew and Helby to bring Donald Litton to Redbourn police station again for further questioning. There was no objection from either the boy or his mother. On the way he asked Askew, 'What do you want me down there again for?' When Askew replied, 'There are certain factors in your statement to us which do not agree with the statement you made to Mr Ford,' Litton calmly said, 'If I tell the truth shall I get summoned?' Askew then cautioned him but Litton continued, 'My only worry is if my mother gets to know, but I have got it on my mind and wish to get it off. I killed Mrs Seabrook.'

On arriving at the police station at 8.30 p.m., Litton wrote his statement in his own hand, without any prompting from the police officers present, save to express that he had been cautioned.

Redbourn Police Station
February 2nd
I Donald Litton, have been cautioned by Inspector Crutchet and wish to make the following statement to clear my mind:- On the 27th January I went up the garden and came back just after 2 o'clock. My mother had just gone out. She had locked the front door and had taken the key with her. I wanted some money to go to the Zoo at Easter. I went to the barn and got a hammer and put it in my pocket. I went to Mrs Seabrook's back door and tried it. It was bolted. I pushed up the window which was unfastened. I leaned through the window and pushed the bolt back. Then I pulled the window down and opened the door. I looked in the kitchen and front room but I couldn't find any money. I went upstairs into the back room. There was no-one there. I opened the other door slowly and looked in. Mrs Seabrook was lying on the bed. I went in and looked on the table. There was no money. I went into the back room again. Then Mrs Seabrook woke up and saw the door open. She got out of bed and came to the door and saw me. I was very frightened and I struck at her with the hammer. Then I ran downstairs and up the garden and buried the hammer in Miss Weston's garden behind the barn. I came back and went to her house again. She was coming downstairs. I pushed

her over and she tried to get up and I struck her with the poker. The chair fell on the fire. I ran out and got down the well. I didn't hardly know what I was doing. I thought I would try and drown myself. I got down by pressing my feet and back against the opposite sides of the well. When I got to the water I let myself fall. As soon as I got in the water I struggled and got my feet against one wall and my back against the opposite one. I got up like this and went into the house. I took all my clothes off and put them in a small pail. I put them in the kitchen then I sat in front of the fire. At 3.30 Mrs Freeman came home and knocked at our back window. She called 'Mrs Litton'. I said 'Mother isn't in'. She then went to the wall and called 'Police'. She then went in the house and round past our gate. Then she came back with Mr and Mrs Bradshaw. Then a lot of neighbours and school children came. They stood outside. Then a motor car came and took Mrs Seabrook away. My mother came home at 5 o'clock. I told her I had fallen down the well and when Mr Ford came home I told him so. Nobody knew anything about it except me. I don't think I have any blood on my clothes – (Signed) Donald Litton.

Inspector Crutchet made the boy comfortable and at 10.30 p.m. Deputy Chief Constable Knight arrived at Redbourn police station with Sergeant Herbert of Hertfordshire Constabulary. In their presence and the presence of Litton, Crutchet read the confession. Litton was then taken in a taxi to St Albans police station, arriving after 11 p.m. in thick fog, and charged with the murder. He made no reply. Crutchet later wrote of Litton: 'He seems an intelligent boy and is given an excellent character by his school master and his mother has never noticed anything abnormal about the boy.'

On the same day as Litton made his confession, Sarah Seabrook was being laid to rest in Redbourn churchyard. Her body had lain for two days previously at the home of her son Ethelbert at East Common. Long before the appointed time for the cortège to leave the house, large crowds came to pay their respects. Of them, reportedly some five or six hundred walked behind the hearse to the parish church. Many people were undoubtedly there out of curiosity.

The following day, Thursday 3 February 1921, at 9 a.m., Crutchet, Askew and Helby were digging in Miss Weston's garden. When the hammer was dug up, complete with attached hairs, Litton was taken before an occasional court at St Albans town hall and was remanded to Brixton prison until Saturday 5 February. On the day of the trial a great number of onlookers amassed in the surrounding streets in St Albans, purported to be several hundred people, including many children. From that moment on 6 the Common was kept under police guard, with no inhabitants and Crutchet holding possession of the key.

Dr Bernard Spilsbury, Home Office Pathologist. (Punch)

Litton remained on remand at Brixton prison until, following the inquest, he was committed for trial at the Hertfordshire Assizes on 22 June. Here he appeared before Mr Justice Rowlatt and pleaded 'not guilty'. Born 17 March 1907, Litton was not quite fourteen at the time of the murder and was by law presumed incapable of committing a crime. However, this presumption could be rebutted if it were proven in the course of the evidence that he possessed a discretion to know that he was doing wrong and had criminal intent at the time he was alleged to have murdered Sarah Seabrook.

At the trial his mother proclaimed her son, an only child, was an intelligent boy who got on well at school. He had a close friend, although he never mixed much with the other lads, preferring to confine his attention to fretwork (ornamental designs in wood) as a hobby. He had never caused her any trouble and she knew of no history of insanity either on her or her late husband's side of the family.

Sergeant Askew gave evidence in regard to the boy's confession and Inspector Crutchet stated that the plaster cast of the footprint and Litton's boot perfectly corresponded. Dr Spilsbury spoke of the injuries saying that two or three could have been caused by the old woman falling down the stairs, but the remainder must have been caused by blows delivered by another person. Some of these could have been inflicted with a poker and some with a hammer. His post-mortem evidence pointed to some of the wounds on the head being caused when the deceased was unconscious and unable to move, the assailant standing in one position all the time.

Throughout the hearing Donald Litton was described as 'remarkably self possessed', maintaining a calm demeanour.

In summing up, the coroner observed that Litton, a 'big boy for his age', displayed indications of 'somewhat abnormal intelligence' and described him as not violent but of a rather 'taciturn disposition'.

The judge turned to the jury and asked them to consider the fact that the boy had written his confession himself, that he had initially given a false statement to the police, with no mention of having visited the house of the deceased, and the fact that he had buried the hammer showed that he knew he had done wrong. There could be no question of him being incapable of criminal intention and of the charge being manslaughter; it was murder and nothing else. After three minutes' conference the jury found Litton guilty of 'wilful murder' and the judge ordered him to be detained at His Majesty's pleasure.

After the trial Mrs Litton, forty-four, had an interview with her son, asking him what made him do it. He replied, 'I don't know, Mother, but I am very sorry and mean to make good.' Referring to the question of her son going to Mrs Seabrook's with the intention of robbery, she said that he had asked her for money to go on a zoo trip with the school. She reassured him that she would get the money for him somehow and he had seemed satisfied and happy with her reply. She could not understand what had possessed him to go to Mrs Seabrook's. However, Litton's headmaster maintained that Donald had never mentioned being interested in the trip to the zoo.

Donald Litton was given an assumed name and detained in a reformatory school. The records concerning his detention are closed until 2031. Sarah Seabrook's skull and the poker, however, made a gruesome reappearance in a demonstration given by Dr Spilsbury to the Medico-Legal Society a year after the murder.

18

THE DEEP FREEZE DEATH

Wheathampstead, 1957

Deep mystery surrounds the death of seventeen-year-old Anne Noblett. She alighted from a bus at Cherry Tree Corner, Wheathampstead at about 6 p.m. on Monday 30 December 1957 and was never seen alive again.

Described as a 'happy, normal' teenager, Anne was returning from dancing classes at Lourdes Hall, Harpenden and had said goodbye to friends at around 5.40 p.m., telling them she would see them at the next dance class on Friday. Shortly afterwards her mother had a telephone call from Anne saying that she was in Harpenden and had missed her bus home but would be catching the next one. She said she was bringing home some mushrooms.

The last person to see Anne alive was twenty-one-year-old Shirley Edwards, a poultry worker employed at Marshalls Heath Farm, which was owned by Anne's father. Shirley was leaving work as usual at 6 p.m. and riding her scooter along Marshalls Heath Lane, Wheathampstead on her way home to Robbery Bottom House in Welwyn. She said, 'I saw her [Anne] outside the Cherry Tree public house on the Luton road. She was at the bus stop but whether she was getting on or off a bus I don't know. The time was about three minutes past six. She seemed all right to me. I said "Hello" and that was all. I didn't really take any notice.'

It was a rainy December night and Anne would have had to walk about a quarter of a mile along the lonely unlit Marshalls Heath Lane to her home, Heath Cottage.

Her father, Thomas Noblett, returned home at around 6.40 p.m., having just come from his brother's house where they had been having a business discussion. Anne was not home and his wife said she was expecting her any minute. When she had not arrived by 9 p.m., Mr Noblett became worried and began telephoning her friends. On receiving no news of her he telephoned the police.

The next day, New Year's Eve, police officers with tracker dogs and civilians combed the nearby fields and woods searching for any clues as to what had happened to the teenager. The search ended just before dark, but nothing of relevance had been discovered, except a neighbour who claimed to have heard a scream in the lane around the time of Anne's disappearance. The CID then became involved under the direction of Detective Superintendent Leonard Elwell of Hertfordshire police and the quiet countryside of Marshalls Heath was transformed into an investigation headquarters with police vehicles, caravans, tents and a control room assembled on the grass outside the Noblett house.

When she disappeared Anne had been wearing a charcoal grey reversible raglan coat, a grey flannel skirt and a pale blue knitted cardigan. She was also wearing two-tone spectacles with fashionable 'flyaway' frames. She was five feet eight inches tall and well built with dark hair, grey eyes and a round face.

Within a few days Scotland Yard was called in and 300 soldiers had joined the hunt. Search party numbers were boosted by villagers all anxious to find Anne. Locals could think and talk of nothing else and huddled together in shops and

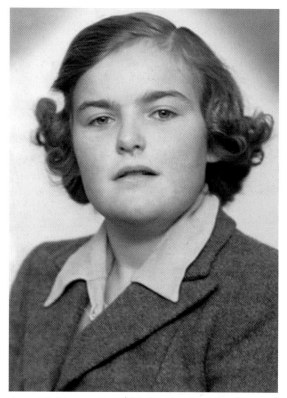

Anne Noblett, a favourite family photograph (Hugh Noblett)

on street corners discussing various theories and possibilities as to what could have happened to the teenager. Among the civilian searchers were numerous men who worked at Helmets Ltd, the Wheathampstead factory where Mr Noblett was director. One employee said, 'Mr Noblett was terribly upset and asked us if we would mind lending a hand. We all willingly volunteered to do so.' Over 1,000 police officers were now employed in the search which had extended to a nine-mile radius around her home.

Mr Noblett stated in the *Hertfordshire Advertiser* on 17 January 1958 that he and his wife had received so many letters of sympathy that they had been overwhelmed. The investigation was given a great deal of help by local firms who had placed vehicles and staff at the disposal of the police and volunteers gave up their weekends to join in the search in awful weather conditions. But the family were also plagued by hoax calls during this time which made the situation even more traumatic.

Anne had returned from a Swiss finishing school near Montreux in July and had enrolled on a domestic science course at Watford Technical College, but her aim was to be a children's nurse. CID officers made enquiries at the college but discovered nothing out of the ordinary. Detective Superintendent Elwell said, 'We are doing everything we possibly can. There is nothing at all in her background to account for her disappearance. She has always seemed very happy.' Anne's brother remembers her as being a great joker, particularly on one occasion when, aged about fourteen, she startled him with a plastic spider, dangling it over his head when he was climbing the stairs at Heath Cottage.

The residents of Marshalls Heath were frightened. They had been appealing to the council for two years for lighting along the lane. One resident described the lane after dark as being 'pitch black, just like going into a forest'. After Anne's disappearance their pleas were stepped up, led by Anne's uncle Leonard Noblett. He told the *Hertfordshire Advertiser* in January 1958, 'Since the recent unfortunate occurrence, there has been considerable agitation for lighting on that spot. People here are afraid to walk around.'

Anne had been learning to drive around the time of her disappearance and it was always her mother's greatest regret that she had not allowed Anne to take the car to Harpenden that December evening. Although it would have been illegal for a learner to drive unaccompanied, Anne would probably have returned home safely.

But despite the massive search, 2,000 people being interviewed, countless cars examined, newsreels at the cinema and appeals in the press both locally and nationally, Anne was not found. That is not until a month later when on 31 January 1958 a young RAF aircraftman stumbled across her body in woodland five miles from the lane where she vanished. Hugh Symonds, twenty-one, and his younger brother Brian were walking their dog on the outskirts of Rose Grove Wood, known locally as 'Young's Wood', Whitwell, when their dog Rip disappeared into some bushes after a rabbit. Hugh followed and there in a clearing ahead of him lay the body of Anne. Hugh stated: 'I came into the clearing and could see the body. I didn't go right up but I could clearly see the legs. It was like someone lying asleep but I knew the person must be dead. We came back to the house and called out the police.'

It was a mild but foggy January afternoon and police vehicles descended on the woodland in force. No attempt had been made to conceal the body. Anne was lying on her back, wearing the clothes she had worn the night she disappeared and with her hands placed gently across her chest. She was even still wearing her glasses, and her purse containing the thirty shillings she had gone out with was found on the ground alongside her.

The police were of the opinion that her body had been taken to the wood by car along one of the many tracks and then carried by the killer or killers to its resting place in the clearing. Anne was larger than average, weighing over eleven stone, and police believed it may have taken two men to carry her the 300 yards through tangled woodland as there was no sign of the body having been dragged. They also surmised that the killer or killers must have had local knowledge as getting to the isolated spot was not easy but the tracks were sometimes used as short cuts by locals in the summer. 'One could not imagine any ordinary vehicle getting down that rutted lane with ease,' said Superintendent Richard Lewis of Scotland Yard.

In an attempt to pinpoint how long the body had lain in the woodland, meteorological staff from nearby Rothamstead Experimental Station went to the spot to check how temperatures in the wood compared to that of the body when it was found. The conclusions were compared with records of temperatures in the area from the date Anne disappeared on 30 December. The results startlingly revealed that Anne's body was very much colder than would have been expected if it had lain for weeks in the open woodland, despite the thin layer of snow that had fallen the week before.

Eminent Home Office pathologist Dr Francis Camps carried out a post-mortem examination and made a further sinister discovery. He concluded that Anne had died of asphyxia due to compression of the neck, but this did not necessarily mean she had been manually strangled. He also revealed that some 'sexual interference' had taken place. The mystery deepened further when the examination also showed that the body had been kept in a condition of deep freeze such as would be caused by it being kept in a refrigerator. Nothing of this sort had ever been known before and police at once set to work checking on all deep freeze equipment within thirty miles of Whitwell, especially poultry keepers and those possessing industrial freezers and others who used 'chillers' for storing meat ready for market.

It appeared unlikely that Anne's body had lain in the woodland for the entire month. Her clothing was still intact and there were no signs of decomposition on the body. Although it was the depths of winter the season had been on the whole unusually wet and mild, as records from Rothamstead Experimental Station confirmed. A gamekeeper stated that he passed the spot every day with his dogs to feed his pheasants and had never seen anything, nor had his dogs ever discovered anything untoward while ferreting in the bushes.

Even more bizarrely, Scotland Yard chiefs had reason to believe that Anne had been stripped then re-dressed after death, as evidenced by the buttons on her underclothes being wrongly done up, a mistake Anne would not have made. The killer had even taken the trouble to replace her spectacles on her nose. There had been no signs of a struggle as none of Anne's clothing had been torn.

House to house enquiries began in earnest. One poultry farmer told police that he remembered seeing a black Austin car parked in the road some distance from the wood the day before Anne's body was discovered. He said it was foggy but he could make out the Hertfordshire registration RUR and the driver was a 'powerfully built' man with horn-rimmed glasses. He was never traced. Another witness said he had seen two red lights in Marshalls Heath Lane shortly after 6 p.m. on the night Anne disappeared. The man had been alighting at the same bus stop where Anne was last seen only minutes earlier. He stood talking to a friend for a few minutes then turned to walk a short distance up the lane before turning off on a footpath leading to the Lea

*Police and civilian
searchers at Marshalls
Heath with a tracker dog.
(Harpenden Free Press)*

Valley estate. He told police that he saw the lights a few hundred yards ahead along the lane but was unsure whether they were those of a car or of two bicycles. People who travelled along the lane twenty minutes later on that dark, rainy evening claim to have seen and heard nothing. Was Anne offered a lift in a car by somebody she knew? Anne's family were adamant that she would not have got into a car with a stranger unless she was forced by someone powerfully built who had overpowered her.

To add to the mystery, Hugh Symonds claimed he had been plagued by anonymous calls just after the body had been discovered, telling him not to cooperate with the police or give any more information.

And then there was the case of the missing mushrooms. Witnesses had seen Anne carrying the bag of mushrooms when she got on the bus at Harpenden but when her body was discovered she seemed to have all her possessions with her except the bag of mushrooms. The mushrooms eventually turned up when two weeks later police appealed in the local newspapers for anyone who had lost mushrooms on 30 or 31 December in the area of Grove Road, Harpenden to come forward.

The press were calling it one of the most sinister crimes of the century but the police were baffled. It seemed that the killer had deposited Anne in a freezer to conceal the time of death but the question underlying the investigation was why her body had been placed in the wood at Whitwell. Perhaps it was because of a report that the press had been running stating that every house within a ten-mile radius of the bus stop at Marshalls Heath would be searched by police and gardens dug up. If the killer was a local person this would have panicked him into getting rid of the body quickly. However, these newspaper reports were later dismissed as 'preposterous and unfounded'. Besides, all houses in the Wheathampstead area had already been visited. But then perhaps the killer thought the recent fall of snow would disguise the fact the body had been kept in a freezer; this would prevent suspicion falling on those with industrial refrigeration equipment and mislead police into thinking Anne was killed in the Whitwell woodland rather than a few yards from her home.

The inquest took place in April 1958, a few days after what would have been Anne's eighteenth birthday. The courtroom was full, most of those present being press representatives. Anne's father was the first witness and he stated that neither his wife nor himself had any knowledge of any male associates of Anne's and that she was very happy living at home. Detective Superintendent Elwell and Superintendent Richard Lewis of Scotland Yard stated that right from the time Anne was reported missing the police had been very active and instigated a major enquiry. Very thorough searches had been made in the area where Anne was last seen and extended over most of the county. Extensive interviews and searches had been carried out but up to that point they had obtained no satisfactory evidence even to allege who had caused the girl's death. Pathologist Dr Camps said that after examination of the stomach contents and additional examinations he ascertained the time of death was considerably less than twelve hours after Anne had left home that afternoon. Anne's stomach still contained the completely undigested meal she had eaten at about 2.30 p.m.; more evidence that her body had been preserved. When asked for his opinion on the cause of death, he stated he could think of no accidental cause nor could he think from the way in which the body was found that the compression on the neck could have been self-inflicted. The jury's unanimous verdict was that Anne was murdered by person or persons unknown.

The irony was that after a long campaign a street lamp was finally provided for the residents of Marshalls Heath Lane on the very day Anne's body was discovered in the woods.

So it appears the police were looking for a local man who had good knowledge of the area, whom Anne knew and who had access to deep freeze equipment, similar to that used for storing poultry. It also suggests that the crime would have to have been planned, as access to a freezer of the size required to store a tall girl lengthways would not have been a common household feature. In 1958 very few domestic freezers were in existence.

Even now, nearly fifty years on, the motive for Anne's death remains elusive. She was described as a home-loving girl who had no known boyfriends and her father said that she always told her parents where she was going. The police believed the killer was known to Anne and Detective Superintendent Elwell was convinced her disappearance took place during the quarter-mile walk across the darkened heath to her home. Seven months after her death cinemas were still showing a newsreel appealing for anyone with any information to come forward and her father employed two private detectives to take up the case. Later in 1958 police investigating the murder of a Dutch teenager Mary Kriek in Essex joined forces with the Hertfordshire investigation. Mary Kriek was found battered to death in a ditch at Boxted in the same month as Anne's body had been discovered. The similarities between this case and Anne Noblett were that both girls were young, had taken a lonely bus ride back after dark and had to walk a little way before reaching home. Two men were arrested in Southend and questioned by Hertfordshire and Essex police and Scotland Yard in connection with both girls' murders but the men were eventually released without charge. One of them turned out to be a refrigeration expert. As with Anne, Mary's killer was never found.

In 1961 Scotland Yard officer Detective Chief Superintendent Richard Lewis was back in Southend after the Essex police came into possession of new facts concerning the Anne Noblett case. The police were anxious to speak to a man who had moved to Belgium. Nothing more appears to have come from this investigation. Then the same year a Sunday paper published a story based on information given to them by an anonymous woman in Watford. She had said that at the time of the murder she had been having an affair with one of the county's most notable and respected people. The affair lasted until August 1960 and this is why she had not come forward before. She claimed to have seen two men at the scene of the murder and could identify them. The police have never revealed the identity of this mysterious witness and it is not known if her evidence was of any help to them.

Twenty years later, following an anonymous tip off, detectives returned to search the spot where Anne's murdered body had been found. A police spokesman said later that no useful information had come to light but that the Noblett case had never been officially closed. The file is still open today and as recently as 1988 police were still investigating new clues.

Today Anne's remains lie in a peaceful corner of St Helen's churchyard in Wheathampstead along with those of her father, who died in 1985, and uncle who died in 2001. Villagers still talk today of the rumour and gossip as to who killed Anne Noblett but the truth of what happened that night in December 1957 has gone to the grave with Anne. Perhaps by this time the killer himself is now dead. However, tantalisingly, someone well placed in the investigation reportedly told a respected journalist in 1958 that the police knew the identity of Anne's killer all along, but simply did not have enough evidence to bring him to justice.

19
HERTFORDSHIRE CONNECTIONS

MARTHA RAY

The story of Martha Ray begins and ends in Elstree where she was born in 1745 or '46. Various sources spell her surname differently as Reay or Wray. She was the daughter of a labourer or small farmer and by the age of sixteen she was an apprentice mantua maker (dressmaker) in Clerkenwell. Martha possessed a fine singing voice which entranced the notorious rake the Earl of Sandwich who installed her as his mistress at his Hinchingbrooke home.

In December 1775 she met twenty-three-year-old Captain James Hackman of the 68th Regiment who was in Huntingdon on a recruiting expedition.

James Hackman and Martha Ray. (Stewart P. Evans)

They corresponded and met but despite his proposals of marriage she would not leave the Earl. Hackman left the army in 1776 and took holy orders, becoming the rector of Wiveton, Norfolk, but he remained obsessed with Martha Ray.

On 7 April 1779 Ray was visiting the Covent Garden theatre to see a play called *Love in a Village*. As Ray was getting into her carriage afterwards James Hackman approached her and drew two pistols from his pockets. He fired at Ray's head, killing her instantly, and then shot himself with the other pistol. Hackman and Ray fell to the ground feet to feet. Hackman's wound was not fatal and he began to beat his head with the gun in a vain attempt to kill himself. An apothecary named Mahon wrenched the gun from Hackman's hand and dressed his wounds.

Hackman's attack and suicide attempt were premeditated. He had written a suicide note to his brother-in-law which read, 'You well know where my affections were placed; and having by some means or other lost her's (an idea which I could not support) has driven me to madness.' He had allegedly used one of Martha Ray's love letters to him as wadding for the pistols.

The body of Martha Ray was returned to Elstree and buried in the churchyard on 14 June. Two days later James Hackman stood trial for her murder at the Old Bailey. He admitted his guilt and addressed the court: 'I stand here this day the most wretched of human beings, and confess myself criminal in a high degree . . . a momentary phrenzy overcame me, and induced me to commit the deed I now deplore.'

Hackman was executed at Tyburn on 19 April before a large crowd which included James Boswell, the biographer of Samuel Johnson. Ballad sheets were published to commemorate the event, one of which read:

> O clergyman! O wicked one!
> In Covent Garden shot her;
> No time to cry upon her God,
> It's hoped He's not forgot her!

Martha's remains appear to have been moved since the date of her interment. When Elstree church underwent repairs in July 1824 her coffin was found in a vault in the centre of the chancel. A gravestone in the churchyard now marks her final resting place. A letter to the editor of *The Times* in 1928 revealed that it was the then present Lord Sandwich who replaced Martha's crumbling tombstone with the one which stands there today.

THOMAS NEILL CREAM

Thomas Neill Cream was born in Glasgow in 1850. His family emigrated to Canada when he was four or five years old. Cream qualified as a doctor in 1876 but favoured a career as an abortionist and blackmailer. The first part of his criminal career ended with a long imprisonment in America for murder.

Upon being released in 1891 Cream came to England, and within a month of arriving he had murdered two Lambeth prostitutes by strychnine poisoning. The following month he was introduced to Laura Sabatini who lived in Chapel Street, Berkhamsted with her mother. Cream quickly proposed marriage to Sabatini who was described as possessing a 'sad-eyed pretty face'. They became engaged either at the end of November or the beginning of December 1891.

On 6 January 1892 Cream visited the Sabatinis in Berkhamsted where he wrote his will, leaving all his property to Laura. He again went to Berkhamsted on 8 April before returning to Lambeth. There he murdered two more prostitutes, came back to Berkhamsted and went to church with Laura.

Cream's final visit to Berkhamsted lasted from 30 April until 3 May 1892. He asked Laura to write several letters at his dictation. The letters falsely blamed a medical student named Walter Harper for the Lambeth murders. Sabatini was instructed to sign them 'Wm H. Murray' who Cream said was a detective in possession of evidence of Harper's guilt.

Cream was eventually arrested and found guilty of murder at the Old Bailey where Laura Sabatini gave evidence against her fiancé. He was executed at Newgate on 15 November 1892.

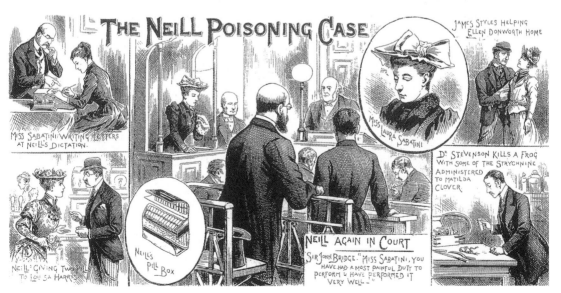

Laura Sabatini from Berkhamsted giving evidence against her serial killer fiancé Dr Thomas Neill Cream. (Illustrated Police News)

GEORGE CHAPMAN

Hertfordshire has been the home to two notable characters who shared the name of George Chapman. The first was the revered Hitchin poet (1559–1634) whose translations of the complete works of Homer remained unsurpassed for centuries. His namesake could not have been more different. He was the nineteenth-century landlord of a Bishops Stortford pub. The veteran crime writer H.L. Adam described him as 'the most cold-blooded monster I ever met'. This George Chapman met his fate on the scaffold one hundred years ago.

George Chapman was not even the landlord's real name. He was born Severin Klosowski in Poland in 1865. At the age of fifteen he was apprenticed to a surgeon and worked as a barber surgeon and hospital assistant. Being of a restless disposition, Klosowski travelled to Warsaw where he enlisted in the Russian army at the age of twenty-one. Eighteen months later he left the army and set sail for England.

Klosowski settled in London where he worked in various establishments as a hairdresser's assistant. In 1889 he married Lucy Baderski, the sister of a Walthamstow tailor. Two years later in 1891 the couple went to live in New Jersey in America but Baderski returned alone in 1892 having tired of her husband's philandering ways. Klosowski soon followed her back to England and they were temporarily reunited before splitting permanently. It was during this marriage that a woman arrived in London from Poland or Russia who claimed to be Klosowski's real wife. She lived with Klosowski and Baderski for a while before returning home.

Klosowski next met and lived with a woman named Annie Chapman. He took her name and became known as George Chapman. They lived together for a year before she left him. In 1895 Chapman courted Mary Isabella Spink who had separated from her husband. Although they were both already married to other people they lived together as man and wife. They opened a barber's shop in Hastings where business began to flourish with the introduction of musical shaves. Spink played a piano while Chapman shaved the customers.

One customer whom Chapman often shaved was a local chemist named William Henry Davidson. Through the course of their conversations Davidson gained an im-

George Chapman. (Notable British Trials)

pression that Chapman possessed a good knowledge of medicines and he readily agreed to sell him one ounce of tartar emetic poison. In Davidson's poisons book Chapman entered his reason for purchasing the poison as what looked like 'take'.

Chapman and Spink returned to London where they took over the Prince of Wales public house. It was here that Spink's health rapidly collapsed and she died on Christmas day 1897. Her death was ascribed to the wasting disease phthisis. Chapman appeared to be grief stricken but still opened the pub at the normal time on the day of Spink's death.

Chapman advertised for a new barmaid and appointed Bessie Taylor, the daughter of a Cheshire farmer, whom he soon 'married' in a bogus wedding ceremony. It is not clear how or where this ceremony took place. No entry appears in the marriage indexes of the General Register Office. The 'bride' seemed convinced that she was genuinely married but Chapman always insisted upon keeping any marriage certificate to himself. The couple moved from the Prince of Wales to Bishops Stortford along with a little boy named Willie, probably the son of Mary Spink. On 25 August 1898 George Chapman became the licensee of the Grapes public house which was located on the corner of South Street and Apton Road. It had originally been a sixteenth-century dwelling that had become a public house in the 1850s.

Shortly before Christmas 1898 Taylor was visited by an old friend named Elizabeth Painter who stayed for three weeks. Painter had known Taylor for seven years and in all that time Taylor had always enjoyed very good health, but at the Grapes Painter found her friend suffering from toothache caused by an abscess.

Taylor went into hospital for the removal of the abscess in her mouth and remained there for about a week. During this time Elizabeth Painter remained at the Grapes with Chapman and got on very well with him. Upon returning from hospital Taylor was still rather unwell and unable to eat solids. Although she could still get about on her own, Taylor's condition did not improve while Painter was there. Painter noticed that Chapman's attitude towards his 'wife' had now changed and he 'wasn't kind to her at all'. He even threatened her with a revolver for having told customers at the Grapes that she was going into hospital.

George Chapman and Bessie Taylor. (Notable British Trials)

Next door to the Grapes was a stable owned by Bishops Stortford bailiff Frederick Thomas Sanderson. He had also noticed that Taylor was in good health when she arrived at the Grapes but had complained about pains in her teeth around Christmas. Sanderson struck up an acquaintance with George Chapman and the pair often engaged in long conversations. Early in 1899 Chapman asked Sanderson where he could obtain forms for his wife to make a will. Sanderson mentioned the names of two stationers' shops that sold them. Chapman immediately departed and returned later that day to show Sanderson a form headed 'This is my last will and testament', explaining that Bessie Taylor wanted to make her will. Sanderson also noticed the change in behaviour of Chapman towards Taylor. He remembered it as 'all right at first, and then very brusque'.

Chapman and Taylor left the Grapes at the beginning of May 1899 and moved to the Monument tavern in London. There, Taylor was described by a neighbour as 'one of the nicest ladies who ever breathed'. She was friendly with the customers, kind to the poor and generally considered to be 'a most superior lady.' Taylor began to waste away while Chapman continued to physically abuse her. She died on 13 February 1901 from 'exhaustion from vomiting and diarrhoea'. She was thirty-six years old. Her death was registered under her bogus married name of Chapman.

Six months later Chapman hired and 'married' another barmaid named Maud Marsh. They moved to the Crown pub in the Borough of Southwark. Marsh suffered an identical fate to Mary Spink and Bessie Taylor, but this time poisoning was suspected and no death certificate was issued. The doctor explained to Chapman, 'I cannot find what is the cause of death.' Chapman replied, 'It was exhaustion caused by inflammation of the bowels.' The doctor asked, 'What caused the inflammation?' Chapman said, 'Continual vomiting and diarrhoea.' The doctor then enquired, 'What caused the vomiting and diarrhoea?' Chapman made no reply.

A post-mortem was conducted and Marsh's corpse was found to contain significant quantities of poison. The same was the case when the bodies of Spink and Taylor were exhumed.

Chapman was arrested on 25 October 1902. He was tried at the Old Bailey on three counts of murder in March 1903. The motive for the murders was described by H.L. Adam as Chapman's 'idée fixe, the pursuit, the capture, and the destruction of women'. George Chapman was found guilty and sentenced to death. On the day of his execution the flag of the Grapes pub flew at half mast. A large crowd of mostly women had gathered outside the prison to await news of the murderer's death. Rumours began to circulate that Chapman was also wanted for a number of murders in Russia and even that he was in fact Jack the Ripper.

If George Chapman had been Jack the Ripper his secret died with him on the scaffold at Wandsworth prison on 7 April 1903. Nevertheless, the crimes of the one-time Bishops Stortford publican place him alongside the Whitechapel fiend in the annals of crime.

The Grapes finally closed for business in 1966.

SAMUEL HERBERT DOUGAL

After twenty-one years in the army Samuel Herbert Dougal returned to civilian life. Dougal was a philanderer. Twice widowed, he had a number of children both legitimate and illegitimate. After trying his hand at several jobs the future 'Moat Farm Murderer' arrived in Hertfordshire early in 1889 and became the landlord of the Royston Crow pub in Baldock Street, Ware.

Dougal was the pub's sixth landlord in five years. He was thought to be a respectable character and Police Sergeant Merchant said that his 'character and antecedents were very good, for if he had not had a first-class character he would not have been granted a licence by the Ware Magistrates'. However, the new landlord proved to be something of a whited sepulchre.

On 3 August Dougal locked up the empty pub at 11.45 p.m. and went to London. Twenty minutes later the premises were ablaze. Dougal returned to Ware two days later to find his pub in ruins. 'It is a bad job about your house,' a local policeman commiserated. 'I can't understand it,' came Dougal's reply.

The insurance company's inspectors believed the fire had been started deliberately by Dougal who was arrested and tried for arson and attempting

Samuel Herbert Dougal flanked by two police officers after his arrest. (Stewart P. Evans)

to defraud his insurance company. The contents of the pub were insured for £650 although they were only worth about £100. Dougal had made a claim for £142 2s 1d which did not seem too excessive and the prosecution were unable to prove that he had definitely set fire to the pub. The jury had no option but to find Dougal not guilty.

Dougal left Hertfordshire and later married a third time. He failed to hold down a steady job and began resorting to crime. In 1895 he was tried and acquitted for larceny. A year later he was found guilty of forgery at the Old Bailey and sentenced to twelve months' hard labour. When Dougal made a failed attempt to commit suicide in prison he was certified insane and served the rest of his sentence in a lunatic asylum. Dougal separated from his third wife and in 1898 he met spinster Camille Holland who was older than him and had a legacy of six or seven thousand pounds.

Miss Holland succumbed to Dougal's blandishments and together they moved to Saffron Walden in Essex in 1899 where people took them to be husband and wife. Dougal often returned to Hertfordshire and went drinking in Bishops Stortford. It has been suggested that he drank in the Grapes when George Chapman was the landlord.

From Saffron Walden the couple moved to Moat Farm in Clavering. Dougal remained a familiar figure in Bishops Stortford. He was one of the few people in the area to own a car and he frequently drove into town in what he called his 'loco-mobile'. Dougal employed a domestic servant from Bishops Stortford called Florence Havies. She had only worked at the farm for one day when Dougal crept up on her in the scullery and kissed her. On her third day there Dougal tried to force his way into her bedroom. She wrote to her mother who quickly took her away to her new home at Swanfield Road, Waltham Cross. Florence Havies was the last person to see Camille Holland alive.

People noticed Holland had not been seen for a long time and rumours spread that Dougal had killed her and buried her on the farm where all her possessions remained. Dougal in the meantime lived at the farm with a string of mistresses and, if the stories are to be believed, gave cycling lessons to naked women in one of his fields.

It was not until 1903 that Essex police interviewed Dougal about Holland's disappearance, during which time he had been forging her signature on cheques. The day after his visit from the police Dougal hurried to Bishops Stortford and withdrew his £300 savings from the London & County Bank in North Street. The body of Camille Holland was dug up on 27 April 1903 in a drainage ditch at Moat Farm. Damage to her skull indicated she had been shot. Florence Havies returned to the farm to identify the clothing of her former mistress.

Samuel Dougal was found guilty of murdering Camille Holland at the Essex Assizes and was sentenced to hang. Ironically Dougal had once applied for the job of hangman but had been rejected. He was executed on 14 July 1903, the same year as George Chapman.

DR CRIPPEN

On 13 July 1910 human remains were discovered buried in the cellar of 39 Hilldrop Crescent, London. The mystery of the whereabouts of Cora Crippen was solved. Her husband, Dr Hawley Harvey Crippen, had fled on a steamer bound for Canada with his young mistress Ethel Le Neve who was disguised as a boy and masquerading as Crippen's son. Scotland Yard were in hot pursuit in a faster boat.

While the world's press reported on the dramatic transatlantic chase, a Liverpool newspaper told of a possible clue in the case from Hertfordshire. Mrs Austin, landlady of the White Horse Inn, Albert Street, Stevenage, had recently answered an advert placed by Crippen respecting a cure for deafness.

The execution of Dr Crippen at Pentonville Prison. Ellis the hangman later carried out two executions at St Albans. (Illustrated Police News)

151

She had received several typewritten communications from Crippen who was by now little more than a quack doctor.

Mrs Austin ordered an instrument from Crippen but was horrified to see an account of his crime in that evening's newspaper. She rushed to the bank to cancel her cheque for the order but it arrived the following week. The accompanying postcard was not written by Crippen but nevertheless Mrs Austin handed the entire package to the police who took the precaution of forwarding it to Scotland Yard.

Crippen was caught before he reached Canada and was brought back to England for trial. He was executed on 25 November 1910 at Pentonville prison for the murder of his wife. The governor of Pentonville prison during Crippen's time there was Major Owen Edward Mytton-Davies who retired to 34 Bowers Way, Harpenden (Elm Lodge) in 1926.

Years later Mytton-Davies recalled Crippen: 'I must admit, owing to the notoriety surrounding his case, as there was nothing heroic about him. He was a sordid, mean, avaricious little man, whose one redeeming feature was his extraordinary devotion to Ethel Le Neve.' Mytton-Davies died in Harpenden in 1934 and was buried in the churchyard.

ALFRED ARTHUR ROUSE

Alfred Arthur Rouse around the time of his marriage. (Notable British Trials)

In 1914 Alfred Arthur Rouse enlisted in the army. Before he was sent to fight in France he married Lily May Watkins at St Saviour's church, St Albans on 29 November 1914. He was three years younger than his Clerkenwell bride and gave his address as 1 Sandpit Lane, St Albans. Rouse attained the rank of major in the army but his military career was cut short when he received severe injuries to his head, thigh and leg when he was caught in a shell burst. He was discharged in 1916 and deemed unfit for active service.

Rouse became a commercial traveller and his good looks and smooth talk ensured he was a success. He travelled around the country and became involved with as many as eighty different women. Then there was a bigamous marriage and several illegitimate children whom he had to support. Life was becoming too complicated and expensive. Not surprisingly Rouse decided that he 'wanted to start afresh'.

In 1930 Rouse and his long-suffering wife were living in Barnet. As Guy Fawkes Night approached Rouse hatched a plan which he hoped would put an end to his troubles. He got talking to a 'down and out' in Whetstone High Road. The man told Rouse he was looking for work and had no relatives. 'He was the sort of man no one would miss, and I thought he would suit the plan I had in mind,' recalled Rouse. This plan was to kill the man and burn the body in his car so that it was believed Rouse had died in the fire. He could then start a new life for himself. They arranged to meet again on 2 or 3 November and Rouse told him that he was going to Leicester on 5 November and offered him a lift so he might look for work there.

When that day arrived Rouse duly picked the man up and drove northwards. Rouse wanted to commit the murder as late at night as possible so he stopped the car about a mile from Markyate in Watling Street, St Albans at around 11.15 p.m. PC David Lilley, who was stationed at Markyate, was on cycle patrol that night. He saw Rouse's car pull up in front of him just past the White Flag tearoom. Rouse's passenger accidentally switched off the car's lights and Lilley stopped to check on the car and saw that there was a passenger in it. Rouse apologised, turned the lights back on and drove off.

In the early hours of 6 November Alfred Rouse stopped his car in a quiet lane in Hardingstone near Northampton. He strangled his passenger who was by then drunk from the bottle of whisky his killer had given him. Rouse then set fire to the car hoping that a fire that night would be less conspicuous. He believed that 'it was possible to beat the police if you were careful enough', but Rouse was seen walking away from the burning car. This along with other circumstantial evidence led to Rouse's arrest in London. His initial story to the police was that he had picked the man up on the Great North Road, 'just this side of St Albans'.

Rouse was tried for murder at the Northampton Assizes where he was found guilty. His wife moved from Barnet and got a job as a shop assistant in Northampton so she could be near him during his last few weeks. She stood by him until the end saying that her 'own opinion is that he was not in his right mind on November 5'. Rouse was executed at Bedford on 10 March 1931. His victim was never identified.

Appendix 1

JACK THE RIPPER'S HERTFORDSHIRE

Jack the Ripper remains the most infamous murderer in history despite his identity being a perpetual mystery. Surviving Scotland Yard files list eleven murders of impoverished East London prostitutes between April 1888 and February 1891. How many of these women were murdered and mutilated by the same hand is not known today and was a matter of contention at the time. All the murders remain unsolved but many people were suspected and arrested, including a number with Hertfordshire connections.

The sixth Whitechapel murder victim, Catherine Eddowes, was horrifically slain in Mitre Square which was within the jurisdiction of the City of London police. On duty that night was Hertfordshire native Detective Constable Daniel Halse.

Daniel Halse was born on 19 May 1842 at Home Park Cottages, Abbots Langley and was eventually baptised in 1846 at Bovingdon church. His father Thomas had worked as a paper maker for over twenty years with the same company. Thomas got his son a job as a paper stainer at the mill in 1855. Halse worked there until 1863, when he applied to join the City of London police. The vicars of Abbots Langley and Kings Langley both gave Halse good character references and he gained admission to the police force of the square mile which was independent from the Metropolitan police. Halse stood 5 feet 8 inches tall with brown eyes, dark hair and dark complexion. He moved to London and married in 1875. By 1888 he was a detective constable.

Just before 2 a.m. on Saturday 30 September Halse was with colleagues detectives Outram and Marriott by Aldgate church. They heard that a woman had been murdered in Mitre Square. The three men rushed to the square where one look at the remains of Catherine Eddowes made it all too obvious she had met her death at the hands of Jack the Ripper.

Halse gave instructions for the neighbourhood to be searched and every man found to be examined. He set off down Middlesex Street into Wentworth Street where he stopped two men but released them after they gave satisfactory accounts of their presence there. Halse returned to Mitre Square via Goulston Street at 2.20 a.m. but saw nothing untoward.

From Mitre Square Halse went to the mortuary where he witnessed Eddowes's corpse being stripped. He noticed that part of her apron was missing. The missing piece of apron had been found by PC Alfred Long at

2.55 a.m. in Goulston Street where Halse and Long had passed earlier and seen nothing. The apron was the only tangible clue to be found in connection with any of the murders, for it indicated the direction the Ripper had fled from Mitre Square after murdering Catherine Eddowes.

The apron had been discovered in the entry to the staircase of a block of flats. Halse observed that some words had been chalked on the black fascia of the wall in a good schoolboy hand. It read, 'The Juwes are The men that Will not be Blamed for nothing.' Halse noted the message down and thought it had been written recently because if any of the Jewish inhabitants of the tenements had seen it they would have rubbed it out.

Halse stood guard by the message while a colleague sought instructions from a superior officer to have the message photographed. As dawn approached traders began setting up their stalls and there were fears that if the message was seen it could lead to riots and violence against the large Jewish population of East London. Metropolitan Police Commissioner Sir Charles Warren ordered the message to be rubbed out before it could be photographed. Halse suggested that just the top line of the message be erased but he was overruled and the whole message was rubbed out at around 5.30 a.m.

The Whitechapel murders reached a pinnacle of horror with the murder of prostitute Mary Kelly in her squalid room in Miller's Court on 9 November. The autumn of terror was over but four more women were murdered between December 1888 and February 1891, each time reviving the panic that Jack the Ripper had returned.

Thus ended Jack the Ripper's reign of terror. Hundreds of men had been questioned and come under suspicion for the flimsiest of reasons. In 1894 the Assistant Chief Constable of the CID, Sir Melville Macnaghten, wrote a report naming three Scotland Yard suspects, two of whom had links with Hertfordshire.

One of the suspects was Michael Ostrog whom Macnaghten described as 'a Russian doctor, and a convict, who was subsequently detained in a lunatic asylum as a homicidal maniac. This man's antecedents were of the worst possible type, and his whereabouts at the time of the murders could never be ascertained.'

Before achieving notoriety as a Ripper suspect Michael Ostrog was a well-known figure in the criminal courts and gaols of the English shires. He was first heard of in Oxford in 1863 when he was sentenced to ten months' hard labour for a series of thefts from the university while masquerading as a German student under one of his numerous aliases.

Within weeks of his release Ostrog appeared in Bishops Stortford. He introduced himself to a respectable tradesman as Count Sobieski, a fallen Polish nobleman who had escaped from Warsaw after being sentenced to exile in Siberia. He was making his way to Cambridge (which he pronounced as 'Camber witch') to join some of his countrymen who were studying there. Ostrog said he required accommodation but as he only had 1s 8d it would

The Coach and Horses, Bishops Stortford, where Ripper suspect Michael Ostrog lodged in the 1860s. (HALS CV 360)

have to be 'not grand'. The tradesman took Ostrog to the neighbouring Coach and Horses hostelry. Ostrog's 'plausible manner and pitiable tale touched the sympathies of mine host', and he was given the best spare bed for the night. The next morning Ostrog was told he had nothing to pay for his stay and was given a gold coin to help him get to Cambridge.

Ostrog went to thank the tradesman and tell him of his good fortune. In the tradesman's shop Ostrog spoke to two professional men whom he regaled with his tale and this resulted in his being asked to stay at the house of one of them. There, his 'melancholy story, well-bred and amiable manners, made a friend in the mistress as well as the master, and he became "the star of the house" for four days, when he "reluctantly tore himself away", but not without taking further opportunity of adding to his obligations by the loan of two or three sovereigns'. Ostrog took further advantage of his host by asking him to procure a first-class railway ticket to Cambridge for he feared that his English was not good enough to be understood at the ticket office.

At Cambridge Ostrog told Herbert Draper of Magdalene College his tale of woe, saying he had tramped from Ipswich to Cambridge. He was given accommodation and a sovereign. He returned to Bishops Stortford where he attended church on Sunday. Even within the hallowed walls of St Michael's Ostrog would not pay his own way. He borrowed a piece of silver so that he could contribute to the church restoration fund as he wanted to be a 'charitable Christian'.

Back in Cambridge Draper was becoming suspicious of Ostrog and spoke to Superintendent Turrall about him. Turrall knew something about Ostrog and arrested the scoundrel at Cambridge station when he returned there. Ostrog was sentenced to three months for defrauding Mr Draper. It was reported that Superintendent Ryder of Bishops Stortford would be waiting for Ostrog when he was released from the house of correction to convey him to the Bishops Stortford magistrates' court where he would face charges 'of a more serious character', but this does not appear to have happened.

In the years that followed Ostrog robbed, embezzled and swindled his way throughout many English counties, frequently being arrested and imprisoned. In 1865 he appeared in Gloucestershire where he seemed destitute but was expecting to receive money from a Miss Bourke from Bishops Stortford.

In October 1888 the *Police Gazette* printed Ostrog's picture and warned that 'Special attention is called to this dangerous man'. However, recent research by the historian Philip Sugden shows that Ostrog was in fact in custody in France for most of the Whitechapel murders. Ostrog was last heard of in September 1904 when he was released from Parkhurst prison after serving four years for the theft of a microscope from the London Hospital Medical College.

The head of the Metropolitan CID at the time of the Whitechapel murders was Dr Robert Anderson who made the bold claim that Jack the Ripper had been a local Polish Jew; he had been positively identified as such by a witness who refused to testify against a fellow Jew. Anderson said his suspect was a sexual maniac who had been 'caged in an asylum'.

Anderson's suspect appears to have been a man named as 'Kosminski' by Macnaghten in his memorandum. Macnaghten wrote that Kosminski was 'a Polish Jew, & resident in Whitechapel. This man became insane owing to many years indulgence in solitary vices. He had a great hatred of women, specially of the prostitute class, & had strong homicidal tendencies; he was removed to a lunatic asylum about March 1889. There were many circs connected with this man which made him a strong 'suspect'.'

The likeliest candidate to date is Aaron Kosminski. Nothing is yet known about him during 1888 but in July 1890 he was admitted to Mile End Old Town workhouse and discharged into his brother's care three days later. Kosminski was readmitted to the workhouse in February 1891 and committed to Colney Hatch lunatic asylum in Barnet the same month. His medical certificate stated that:

He declares that he is guided & his movements altogether controlled by an instinct that informs his mind; he says he knows the movements of all mankind. . . . [He] goes about the streets and picks up bits of bread out of the gutter & eats them, he drinks water from the tap & he refuses food at the hands of others. He took up a knife & threatened the life of his sister. He is melancholic, practices self-abuse. He is very dirty and will not be washed. He has not attempted any kind of work for years.

In April 1894 Kosminski was described as being 'demented & incoherent'. He was transferred to Leavesden Asylum in Abbots Langley. The asylum, which opened in 1870, was administered by the Metropolitan Asylum Board and was for Metropolitan imbeciles. Unfortunately Kosminski's case notes have not survived prior to 1910 but in the 1901 census he was classified as a lunatic rather than an imbecile. After that date the surviving records describe him as being 'troublesome', occasionally 'very excitable' and 'very obstinate'. He did no work, was untidy but clean and did not respond coherently to simple questions. Case notes recorded that, 'Patient is morose in manner. No sensible reply can be got by questions. He mutters incoherently.' And later, 'Patient merely mutters when asked questions.'

As he reached the end of his life Kosminski suffered from aural and visual hallucinations. In 1918 he was bed-ridden and suffering from diarrhoea. His weight dropped to below seven stone and he was again confined to bed in 1919, this time suffering from swollen feet and then with erysipelas. Aaron Kosminski died on 24 March 1919.

Another patient from Leavesden Asylum was mooted as a potential Jack the Ripper on 3 October 1888 when a letter appeared in the *Daily Telegraph* signed by 'X' of St Albans. He wrote that a lunatic had escaped from Leavesden Asylum the previous year and had since evaded capture. 'X' thought that such a person could be the Whitechapel murderer and wondered if the London authorities had his description.

The lunatic in question was a man named Macdonald and the story of his escape had originally been reported in the *Hertfordshire Advertiser* in September 1887. Macdonald was said to have been a doctor who had practised successfully in India but returned to England when his money ran out. He entered the St Pancras workhouse and when he began to show signs of madness he was transferred to Leavesden.

Macdonald stood 6 feet 2 inches tall, sported dark, bushy whiskers and had dark skin. He had the disturbing habit of shouting almost incessantly. He was not considered dangerous to men but 'would endeavour to take advantage over women' unless they showed no fear. Macdonald had unexpectedly and swiftly escaped into the thick undergrowth of Bricket Wood while taking outdoor exercise with about twenty-five other patients under the supervision of two keepers. The other patients had to be returned to the asylum before a search could commence.

Macdonald had been sighted in two different places. He had asked some people the way to St Albans and also met a man in Lye Lane near to Bricket Wood railway station. Macdonald asked the man for a match which he lit and held to the man's face to see who he was talking to. When Macdonald realised the man was not a member of the asylum staff he started talking to him and the man eventually had to make his excuses just to get away from the talkative escapee.

Three days after his escape the police and asylum staff found where Macdonald had been sleeping in Bricket Wood. They supposed that he had been existing on nuts and berries. It was hoped that he would return there but that night Macdonald was seen for the last time near Mount Pleasant before plunging into Black Boy Wood.

The *Hertfordshire Advertiser* stated that there was now no reason for alarm. Macdonald was no longer in the locality and he was not a violent lunatic. Further reassurances appeared in the *Daily Telegraph* in

Robert Cecil, Lord Salisbury of Hatfield House. Salisbury was thrice prime minister, including for the period covering the Whitechapel murders. (HALS D/EGr/36)

response to the letter from 'X'. The medical superintendent of the asylum wrote that during Macdonald's time at the asylum he was 'perfectly quiet and harmless, and certainly had no homicidal tendency'. Macdonald was not heard from again.

At the height of the Whitechapel murders any suggestion as to the identity of Jack the Ripper was listened to. No one was above suspicion to the fear-stricken population or mischievous journalists. Even the prime minister, Hatfield's own Lord Salisbury, was the subject of a ludicrous rumour. In 1890 the *Referee* newspaper reported that there 'is not the slightest "Truth" in the statement that Lord Salisbury concealed Jack the Ripper at Hatfield House on the night of the last Whitechapel murder'.

In October 1888 the *Hertfordshire Advertiser* ran a story under the headline 'The Whitechapel Murders. A Suspicious Man at Harpenden'. A rumour was circulating throughout Harpenden that Jack the Ripper 'had made Harpenden his abiding place for a brief period, and had exhibited his murderous knives to the gaze of an affrighted townsman'. The *Advertiser's* representative set out to investigate these worrying claims.

The man in question had turned up in Harpenden looking for accommodation for four months. He said he was a government surveyor named

William Arthur Wills but he later told people that his name was Williams. One day he went for a walk with a man called Robert Locke. They encountered a knife seller and Williams bought a penknife. When the seller had gone Williams told Locke that 'he did not need anything of the sort as he had plenty'. To prove his point Williams drew a black box from the side pocket of his coat. It contained lancets, knives, scissors and keys, all packed in wadding.

Williams appeared to be well versed in anatomy. His normal conversation was divided between surgical and religious topics. He seemed to know a great deal about the Whitechapel murders and remarked that, 'If anybody could find that murderer, I know I could.' Williams made the claim that he had seen the bodies of all of the Ripper's victims from which he formed the opinion that they had been cut up by a doctor and placed where they were found. One of the daughters of Williams's landlord was convinced that this strange new lodger was Jack the Ripper.

Fortunately for the inhabitants of Harpenden it turned out that Williams was no more than a mountebank. He told his landlord that he had to go to Luton to collect £150. The landlord was instructed to wait for Williams on the railway platform that evening. Williams never appeared. He had left without paying any of his bills.

On the same day that the *Hertfordshire Advertiser* told the story of Williams the *Hertfordshire Mercury* had its own story about Jack the Ripper. However, the story proved to be a red herring, the result of a newspaper feeding frenzy for any story about the Red Terror of East London. The Press Association had been circulating a story of a man having been arrested in Bishops Stortford in connection with the murders. Upon further investigation the *Mercury* established that the arrest had never been made. The story was a hoax, probably the result of a 'penny-a-liner' duping the Press Association.

A definite arrest was made on 24 November in Rickmansworth: a man answering the circulating description of Jack the Ripper which was based upon possible sightings of the murderer. The man was arrested in Maple Cross and behaved in 'a most excited manner'. Any hopes that Jack the Ripper had finally been caught were dashed when the man, who was identified as a travelling hawker named Frederick Chapman, appeared at the Watford magistrates' court. He was charged with being drunk and disorderly. Chapman had got into an argument with a fellow drunkard in the George pub. He had been carrying an astonishing sum of £229 16s 5½d in his pocket. Chapman readily admitted he had drunk too much that night and was ultimately fined 5s and ordered to pay costs of 8s 6d.

All of the scares in Hertfordshire were false alarms. Daniel Halse retired from the City of London police in August 1891 and died in February 1894, with the identity of Jack the Ripper being as much a mystery to him then as it remains to us today.

EXECUTIONS FOR MURDER IN HERTFORDSHIRE 1735 – 1914

The list overleaf represents all the executions in Hertfordshire for murder from 1733 when records were first written in English until 1914, the date of the last execution in Hertfordshire. The information was gathered from Ken Griffin's Hertfordshire Assizes Database and David Mossop's *Hertfordshire Death Sentences and Executions 1735–1804* (Cambridge, 2002).

The execution of John Thurtell at Hertford, 9 January 1824. (HALS Pierce Egan's Account)

NAME OF FELON	NAME OF VICTIM	MURDER PLACE	MURDER DATE	EXECUTION DATE
William Morgan	Daniel Hall[†]	Rickmansworth	17.8.1735	22.3.1736
Michael Barber	Daniel Hall (aid & abetting)	Rickmansworth	17.8.1735	22.3.1736
Richard Pilgrim	William & Mary Woodland	Knebworth	12.10.1741	March 1742
Joseph Sell	Margaret Edwards	Standon	1.10.1744	March 1745
Richard Sloper	Thomas Batchelor	Flamstead	2.9.1750	25.3.1751
Thomas Colley	Ruth Osborn	Tring	22.4.1751	24.8.1751
Charles Smith	Thomas Smith (son)	St Albans	31.12.1751	18.3.1752
Thomas Hurry	Alice (bastard daughter)	Northaw	1.12.1751	18.3.1752
Alice Andrew	Alice (bastard daughter)	Northaw	1.12.1751	18.3.1752
Alice Whitman	female bastard	St Albans	11.1.1754	11.3.1754
Isaac Shuffle	Francis Prior	Ware	26.2.1755	10.3.1755
Thomas Wood	Francis Prior (aid & abetting)	Ware	26.2.1755	10.3.1755
William Staines	Mary Morgan	Harpenden	7.4.1757	27–29.7.1757
Daniel Ginger	James Nutkins	Shenley	5.7.1760	11.3.1761 (date set by execution order)
William Passell	Richard Burgess	Bramfield	4.11.1772	13.3.1773
John Wade	Martha Wade (wife)	Little Hormead	10.3.1791	1.8.1791
Ann Mead	Charles Proctor	Royston	16.6.1800	31.7.1800
John Harris	Ben Stapps	Hemel Hempstead	24.9.1806	9.3.1807
Thomas Simmons	Sarah Hummerstone	Hoddesdon	20.10.1807	7.3.1808
Sarah Cock	male bastard	Aston	13.2.1815	18.3.1816
Daniel Munn	John Payne	Studham	1.5.1817	28.7.1817
John Thurtell	William Weare	Aldenham	24.10.1823	9.1.1824
Thomas Darby	William Radley	Eastwick	6.7.1835	20.7.1835
George Fletcher	William Bennett	Tewin	25.10.1837	14.3.1838
William Roach	William Bennett	Tewin	25.10.1837	14.3.1838
Thomas Taylor	William Bennett	Tewin	25.10.1837	13.3.1839
George Hill	William Thrussell	St Albans	4.7.1875	10.4.1876
Thomas Wheeler	Edward Anstee	Sandridge	22.8.1880	29.11.1880
Mary Ann Ansell	Caroline Ansell	Watford	14.3.1899	19.7.1899
Charles Coleman	Rose Ann Gurney	Rickmansworth	15.7.1911	21.12.1911
George Anderson	Emily Whybrew	Waltham Cross	30.6.1914	23.12.1914

† Hall was attacked in Rickmansworth on 14 August and died in Watford three days later.

BIBLIOGRAPHY

Abbreviations
HALS – Hertfordshire Archives and Local
Studies
PRO – Public Record Office

Some Hertfordshire Tragedies
HALS, D/EX 652/43
HALS, Gerish, W.B., *Some Hertfordshire
Tragedies*, manuscript, Bishops Stortford,
1913
Gentleman's Magazine
Cockburn, J.S. (ed.) *Calendar of Assize
Records Hertfordshire Indictments
James I*, London, 1975
Gerish, W.B. *The Surprising Discovery of
Murtherers*, Bishops Stortford, 1915
Urwick, William, *Nonconformity in Herts*,
London 1884

The Trial of Spencer Cowper
Hertford, 1699
HALS, D/EGr/43
Birkenhead, Earl of, *Famous Trials of
History*, London, 1926
Howell, T.B., *A Complete Collection of
State Trials*, volume 13, n.d.
Munby, Lionel M., *The Common People
Are Not Nothing*, Hatfield, 1995
Stephen, H.L. (ed.), *State Trials Political
and Social* volume 2, London 1899
Hertfordshire Countryside, Autumn 1952

The Gubblecote Witch Killing
Tring, 1751
HALS, D/EGr/76
HALS, D/ELw/Z22/13
HALS, D/EP/F272
Hertfordshire Advertiser and St Albans Times
Hertfordshire Mercury
Watford Observer
Hertfordshire Countryside, October 1994
Gentleman's Magazine

Evans, Lewis, Witchcraft in Hertfordshire,
(from Andrews, William (ed.), *Bygone
Hertfordshire*, London, 1898
Knapp, Andrew and Baldwin, William (eds),
The Newgate Calendar, London, 1825

Death of a Highwayman
Bramfield, 1782
HALS, D/ECu/3
HALS, D/EGr/19
HALS, Gerish, W.B., *Dictionary of
Hertfordshire Biography*
*Hertfordshire Advertiser and St Albans
Times*
Hertfordshire Guardian
Hertfordshire Mercury
Gentleman's Magazine
Beachcroft, T. and Emms, W.B., *Five Hide
Village*, Datchworth, 1987
Branch Johnson, W., *Memorandums for . . .
the diary between 1798 & 1810 of John
Carrington*, London, 1973.
*East Herts Archaeological Society
Transactions*, Vol VII, Pt. 4, 1927
Hertfordshire Countryside

The Night of the Double Murder
Hoddesdon, 1807
HALS, 71074, 71118, 71173
HALS, D/EGr/49
HALS, D/ESa 97
HALS, Hine Collection volume 49
PRO, PROB 11/1472
Fairburn's Edition of the Trial of Thomas
Simmons, London, 1808
Christie, O.F. (ed.), *The Diary of the Revd.
William Jones 1771–1821*, London, 1929

The Sensational Crime of Regency England
Aldenham, 1823
HALS, 46883H, 63789, 70156
HALS, D/EBk C60/1&3

HALS, D/EGr/28
HALS, D/EHx/11/8, Z32, Z54
HALS, D/ESa 97
HALS, D/P 36/1/17
Farmers' Journal
Globe and Traveller
Hertfordshire Advertiser and St Albans Times
Hertfordshire Mercury
The Observer Colour Supplement
St Albans Review
Sunday Express
The Times
Watford Observer
Borowitz, Albert, *The Thurtell-Hunt Murder Case*, London, 1988
Watson, Eric R. (ed), *Trial of Thurtell and Hunt*, Edinburgh and London, 1920
Hertfordshire Countryside
Hertfordshire Past and Present Vol. II, 1961
Unless otherwise stated the illustrations for the Thurtell chapter are taken from:
Anonymous, *A Complete History and Development of all the Extraordinary Circumstances and Events Connected With the Murder of Mr Weare*, London, 1824
Anonymous, *The Fatal Effects of Gambling Exemplified in the Murder of William Weare*, London, 1824
Egan, Pierce. *Account of the Trial of John Thurtell and Joseph Hunt*, London, 1824
Jones, George Henry, *Account of the Murder of the Late Mr William Weare*, London, 1824

A Triple Hanging
Tewin, 1837
HALS, D/P 106/10/1
HALS, *Hertford Gaol Governor's Journal 1834–1837*
HALS, QSR 66
PRO, ASSI 94/2252
PRO, ASSI 94/2723
PRO, HO 17/56
County Press
County Reformer

Morning Advertiser
Morning Chronicle
The Times
Bryant, G.E. (ed.) and Baker, G.P. (ed.), *A Quaker Journal* vol. 1, London, 1934

Death in the Line of Duty
Stevenage, 1857, Benington, 1871
HALS, D/ESa 97
PRO, ASSI 36/9
PRO, ASSI 36/17
PRO, ASSI 37/2
PRO, ASSI 40/1
Hertfordshire Mercury
St Albans Times
Hertfordshire Constabulary Souvenir Brochure 1841–1991
Hertfordshire Past Vol. 32, 1993
Ashby, Margaret, *Stevenage Past*, Chichester, 1995
Osborn, Neil, *The Story of Hertfordshire Police*, Letchworth, 1970
Hertfordshire Advertiser and St Albans Times

The Green Lane Baby Killer
St Albans, 1875
HALS, *Hertford Gaol Governor's Journal 1875–1878*
HALS, SH 2/4/3
Hertfordshire Advertiser and St Albans Times
Hertfordshire Mercury
The Times
Watford Observer

Murder at Marshalls Wick
Sandridge, 1880
HALS, SH2/4/1
Hertfordshire Advertiser and St Albans Times
Review & Express
St Albans Review
The Times
Carrington, Beryl & Richardson, Robert, *Yesterday's Town*, Oxford, 1986
Dunk, Geoff, *Around St Albans with Geoff Dunk*, St Albans, 1985

Guilty or Insane?
Elstree, 1882
HALS, SH2/4/2
PRO, MH 94/27
Barnet Press, Finchley News & Edgware
Chronicle
Hertfordshire Mercury
Hertfordshire Standard and St Albans
Citizen

The Hertford Horror
Hertford, 1899
Hertfordshire Advertiser and St Albans
Times
Herts & Cambs Reporter & Royston Crow
Hertfordshire Mercury
Watford Observer
Hertford Oral History Group, *Children of*
the Angel, London, 1998

Murder at the Asylum
Abbots Langley, 1899
HALS, SH2/4/2
PRO, HO 144/277/A61150/(1-79)
Daily Mail
Hemel Hempstead Gazette
Hertfordshire Advertiser and St Albans
Times
Hertfordshire Standard and St Albans
Citizen
Illustrated Mail
Watford Observer
Whittington-Egan, Molly, *Doctor Forbes*
Winslow Defender of the Insane, Great
Malvern, 2000
Winslow, L. Forbes, *Recollections of Forty*
Years, London 1910

A Love Tragedy
London Colney, 1910
HALS, Off Acc 1025
Hertfordshire Advertiser and St Albans
Times
Illustrated Police News

The Last Hertfordshire Hanging
Waltham Cross, 1914
HALS, SH 2/4/2

Hertfordshire Advertiser and St Albans
Times
Hertfordshire Mercury
Herts and Essex Observer

The Shop Murder Mystery
Hitchin, 1919
PRO, MEPO 3/260
Hertfordshire Express
Herts & Cambs Reporter & Royston
Crow
Thomson's Weekly Newspaper

A 'Rum Affair'
Redbourn, 1921
PRO, HO 144/11820
PRO, MEPO 3/286
Hertfordshire Advertiser and St Albans
Times
Hertfordshire News & County Advertiser
The Times
West Herts and Watford Observer

The Deep Freeze Death
Wheathampstead, 1957
Harpenden Free Press
Hertfordshire Advertiser and St Albans
Times
Hertfordshire Express
St Albans Observer
Stevenage Gazette
The Times
Weekend
West Herts and Watford Observer
Jackson, Robert, *Francis Camps Famous*
Case Histories of the Celebrated
Pathologist, London, 1975
Hugh Noblett – private information

Hertfordshire Connections
Martha Ray
HALS, Acc 3556
HALS, D/EGr/28
HALS, D/P 36/1/2
Hertfordshire Mercury
The Times
Watford Observer
Gentleman's Magazine

Thomas Neill Cream
Illustrated Police News
Shore, W. Teignmouth (ed.), *Trial of Neill Cream*, Edinburgh and London, 1923

George Chapman
PRO, CRIM 1/84
East Herts and West Essex News
Herts and Cambridge Reporter
Herts and Essex Observer
Hertfordshire Mercury
Thomson's Weekly News
Adam, H.L. (ed.), *Trial of George Chapman*, Edinburgh and London, 1930

Samuel Herbert Dougal
HALS, PS 18/3/2
Hertfordshire Mercury
Jesse, F. Tennyson (ed.), *Trial of Samuel Herbert Dougal*, Edinburgh and London, 1928

Dr Crippen
Hertfordshire Advertiser and St Albans Times

Liverpool Courier
Young, Filson (ed.), *Trial of H.H. Crippen*, Edinburgh and London, 1920

Alfred Arthur Rouse
Normington, Helena (ed.), *Trial of Alfred Arthur Rouse* Edinburgh and London, 1931

Appendix 1
Jack the Ripper's Hertfordshire
Corporation of London Records Office, Accn/2001/206/ Box 291/ Halse, D.
Daily Telegraph
Hertfordshire Advertiser and St Albans Times
Hertfordshire Mercury
Herts and Essex Observer
Watford Observer
Evans, Stewart P. & Skinner, Keith, *The Ultimate Jack the Ripper Sourcebook* London, 2000
Sugden, Philip, *The Complete History of Jack the Ripper* revised edition, London, 2002

INDEX